Praise for The Human Climate

"Humankind faces enormous challenges. evidence, many react with skepticism, a result, the physical climate declines, a worsens. What can we do to make the human climate less adversarial, less hateful, less scared and scary? Carol Smaldino's must-read book is life-saving for humankind. She is among the world's few voices focusing on the dark sides of the human soul, its shadow. Only by understanding and befriending our shadow can we heal the climate, both human and physical."

–Evelin Lindner, MD, PhD, founding president, Human Dignity
and Humiliation Studies, Nobel Peace Prize nominee

"In an era rife with dangerous divisions in the nation and the world, *The Human Climate* is a must-read for us all. Carol Smaldino's 'talking out loud' in this book had me doing the same—with the book, with myself, and with others. Read this book and prepare to emerge with an awakened curiosity—questions you never before asked, answers you never before envisioned, and a burning desire to do things differently."

–Karen Branan, author of *The Family Tree: A Lynching in Georgia,
a Legacy of Secrets, and My Search for the Truth*

"Carol Smaldino is a psychotherapist who has used her clinical knowledge and expertise to write an original book on the human climate. She applies a developmental perspective to human relationships spanning childhood and adulthood, and to relationships within government and the international scene. This is a very accessible book, free of clinical jargon but packed with clinical insights into the importance of the recognition of emotions throughout human relationships. Smaldino advocates for attunement to one's feelings, self-reflection, and empathy for others

whether they are our children, our adversaries, or world leaders—
all in the service of promoting a peaceful human climate."

—Peter Buirski, PhD, dean emeritus and clinical professor, Graduate
School of Professional Psychology, University of Denver

"Carol Smaldino has written an accessible, highly germane exploration of our emotional and social climates, at once searching and enlightening. She touches central elements of the human condition and what it might take for us to get along better with each other and ourselves. She stimulates engaging reflection on therapy with individuals and society, a sense of inner-outer difficulties and possibilities. A probing and sharing book relevant for the present moment and beyond."

—Michael Eigen, PhD, associate clinical professor of psychology,
New York University, author of *The Challenge of Being Human*

"A passionate, refreshing, and lucid account of how the stuff therapists know about 'feelings' may serve in the creation of a more empathic social and political world. 'Therapy thinking' as presented herein is not a dry, as dust, professional posture but a creative means of entering deeply—at the 'basement level,' to use Smaldino's term—into the lives of others. I like the way direct and robust challenges to certain therapeutic orthodoxies are mounted without punches being pulled. Lastly, there is a quiet humor that pervades the book, which adds to its refreshingly humble approach—no easy answers."

—Andrew Samuels, professor of analytical psychology, University
of Essex, UK, author of *A New Therapy for Politics?*

"This concept-rich, psychologically penetrating exploration of our human climate is a compassionate, fearless look at one of the core issues of our times. 'Can't we all just get along?' is the question Rodney King put in front of our modern-day collective conscience in 1992. Carol Smaldino's commitment to keep that query front and center is a welcome reminder of the task we all face in continuing to deepen and broaden our capacity to do so. If we face that task with the same fierce curiosity, beginner's mind, and awareness of interdependence she conveys here, we're bound to make progress."

—Greg Jemsek, MA, author of *Quiet Horizon:*
Releasing Ideology and Embracing Self-Knowledge

"Carol Smaldino, in *The Human Climate*, helps us recognize how a yearning to belong can tragically, when not recognized and fulfilled, turn into a desperate need that can even lead to extremism. She helps the reader penetrate our tendency to demonize, on all social levels. This is important reading for our time."

—Christian Picciolini, author of *White American Youth*,
cofounder of Life After Hate

"As the son of a Holocaust survivor, I had been witness to the many different moods harbored by my father, and understandably so. But reading this book helped me understand both his and my moods much better. The notion of 'climate' as a way to describe those moods is a wonderful metaphor to help one on the path toward self-improvement. The sprinkling of case studies also helps solidify the message. Thank you for this book."

—Eli Adler, codirector and coproducer of *Surviving Skokie*

"In this compelling volume, Carol Smaldino connects the psychological and sociological crises of the modern era with a seamless and accessible narrative. She demonstrates with clarity and wisdom the connections between our childhoods and family dynamics, on the one hand, and the world we then create, on the other—and between the emotional world of human beings and the material world those humans then manufacture, with either salutary or horrific consequences. Stitching ourselves and our world together will require an appreciation of the brokenness of both, and *The Human Climate* can help us gain that appreciation."

–Tim Wise, author of *White Like Me: Reflections on Race from a Privileged Son*

"I had expected to be excited by Carol's words but not to find myself, albeit reluctantly, looking at my shadows. It takes a good book to do that, one that takes readers gently but firmly by the hand. Personally, I'm taking bets on how long it will be before the expression 'the human climate' is universal. To paraphrase: once said, it cannot be unsaid. It is original and perfect for us and our times."

–Annette Stephens, Australian author of *The Good Little Girl*

"As can be seen in the pages of her book, *The Human Climate*, Carol Smaldino asks nothing from others that she herself has not attempted, delved into deeply, and met with the pain and joy of self-discovery and self-acceptance. Carol's mind is a brilliant one, not only 'dancing' but restless . . . searching, curious, not willing to settle for superficiality or ungenuineness."

–Laura Beecher, PhD, psychologist

"*The Human Climate* is a timely call for healing the conflicts we hold in our hearts as a crucial path to transforming the divisive social conditions in the world. Writing in a lively and exquisitely clear style, the author describes how we can strengthen our mutual growth by cultivating a climate of connection—both internally and externally. This book offers a powerful message of hope for humanity."

–Linda M. Hartling, PhD, director, Human
Dignity and Humiliation Studies

THE
human
CLIMATE

THE
human
CLIMATE

Facing the Divisions Inside Us
and Between Us

CAROL SMALDINO

Dignity Press
WORLD DIGNITY UNIVERSITY PRESS

For inquiries about author visits, in person or via the Internet, please contact Carol at www.thehumanclimate.com.

Published by Dignity Press
16 Northview Ct.
Lake Oswego, OR 97035
www.dignitypress.org

Front cover design by Jessica Stevens
Back cover and interior design by Christy Collins
Author photo by Mark and Grace Kucza

ISBN 978-1-937570-83-5

ePub edition: ISBN 978-1-937570-84-2
Kindle edition: ISBN 978-1-937570-85-9

Library of Congress Control Number: 2018939980

Publisher's Cataloging-in-Publication data
Names: Smaldino, Carol, author.
Title: The Human climate : facing the divisions inside us and between us / Carol Smaldino.
Description: Lake Oswego, OR: Dignity Press, 2019.
Identifiers: ISBN 978-1-93750-83-5 | LCCN 2018939980
Subjects: LCSH: Emotions. | Empathy. | Affect (Psychology) | Self-actualization (Psychology) | Social psychology. | Interpersonal relations. | BISAC: PSYCHOLOGY / Emotions. | PSYCHOLOGY / Interpersonal Relations. | PSYCHOLOGY / General.
Classification: LCC BF575.E55 S63 2018 | DCC 302.1--dc23

Manufactured in the United States
10 9 8 7 6 5 4 3 2 1

Printed on paper from environmentally managed forestry.
See www.lightningsource.com/chainofcustody for certification.

To empathy—
to our receiving it,
to our having it to give

Contents

Acknowledgments

In book acknowledgments, spouses are often thanked last. But I would like begin by thanking Lino, my husband, for supporting me throughout the journey of writing this book. He knew I had it in me, and he has always loved my mind for the way it dances into insights. I begin with Lino also because, during the last months of writing, he took on a very intimate kind of editing assistance. He knew what I meant to say and helped me find the words to say it. I want to thank Lino also for being willing to look beneath the surface, and for weathering plenty of storms with me so we could grow together in our own human climate.

I also thank my editor, Carolyn Bond, whom I think of as a therapeutic partner and a teacher all in one. I thank her for never giving up, even when my tendency to dance nearly took me flying off the page. She was my mentor in integrating my wanderings with the centering the book needed. Carolyn is fiercely loyal to clarity and to paying attention to the reader's experience. At the same time, she has shown tremendous sensitivity and intuition in sensing and respecting what I want to say.

I would like to thank Wendy Jane Carrel, my publicist, who is very much a book shepherd. Wendy is kind and considerate in a way that almost belies her immense competence in book marketing. She has vast personal integrity and is both passionate and sophisticated in reading people, external trends, and possibilities.

I want to thank the talented graphic designer Jessica Stevens for an enjoyable collaborative experience in creating the book's cover. I also thank Christy Collins for her creative and professional contribution to this project on both back cover design and interior design. Her capacity to work so considerately of me and of deadlines was invaluable. My thanks go also to Martha Woolverton for her careful proofreading.

I would also like to thank Evelin Linder, founder of Human Dignity and Humiliation Studies. The staff of this international organization, especially Evelin and the director, Linda Hartling, have offered appreciation, interest, and tremendous support to me and to my work. To Uli Spalthoff, director of operations at Dignity Press, I offer my gratitude for his faith in the book's process and in me, even when my schedule was compromised by illness. My appreciation extends also to Zsuzsa Luckay Mihalcinova, developmental editor at Dignity Press, for her flexibility and care regarding publication details and organization.

To friends who have been supportive of this writing, and of my ideas in general, I offer thanks as well. My thanks and appreciation go especially to Annette Stephens, Betty Simpson, Amalia Luise, Chiara Zanchetta, Mary Fancher, Kirsten Schatz, Scott Tate, Heidi Miller, and Monica Dianda. Craig Stuart has been available for talking and listening through all flavors of moods, doubts, and creative ideas. I especially thank him for traveling with me through my many changes of perspective on the book. Laura Beecher and I have sat with each other in our respective emotional basements, to be sure. Riding through the ups and downs together over many years is testimony to our persistence and our caring. Caryl Schiff-Greatorex has been a wonderful talking partner as we have taken turns offering clarity and acceptance to one another.

I would like to thank those who took the time to read the manuscript and endorse the book. To my mind, in our sometimes frenetic world, where it is easy to be overwhelmed or else absorbed in one's own agenda, those who are willing to remember our interdependence and offer support are treasures.

I want to thank the people who have sought me out for psychotherapy and supervision as well. They have offered me wonderful opportunities to stretch, often together with them, in inspiring if at times challenging ways. To engage with them—they form almost a community of seekers in my mind, though they do not know each other—has made living through tough times more satisfying and less lonely.

I offer thanks to my children and their families: to Paul and his wife, Emily, and my granddaughter Lyra; and to Emma and her husband, Keith, and my granddaughter Riley. They support me and my efforts to get out there, explore, and share.

I hope it is obvious by now that, for me, sharing is a vital part of living. We are born to share, to give and to receive. I am grateful for the opportunity to offer this book to the reader. I hope many conversations between us will follow. If there is anything we drastically need, it is the intention and practice of listening to and learning from each other.

Introduction

The human climate as a concept came to mind one day some years ago as I sat in my office pondering what I was seeing in my therapy practice: young people who were alienated in school and depressed by social pressures to conform. As a psychotherapist who believes in a developmental approach to therapy—for reasons I'll explain later—I surmised that these young people were struggling with divisions within themselves. I began to wonder sadly: We know so much about the importance of authentic ego development, close relationships, and being understood for the development of children and thus of adults as well. Why aren't these principles more available? Why aren't they being taught and practiced more often?

I then looked outward to larger social contexts, since it's my habit to try to connect the dots between matters of personal import I witness in the therapy room and more political matters—since, theoretically, anyway, everything and everyone is connected. What I saw in those larger social contexts was, again, mostly divisiveness. Here too, I realized sadly, all the information we have at hand—made public in books and articles and testimonies—about how to constructively resolve the divisions between us and among us is by and large not being used.

Specifically, I had watched the issue of climate change hit the bulletin boards of emergency and had then been shocked to see the initial concern be replaced by skepticism, resignation, apathy—even protests denying that climate change is caused by humans. To my amazement, not only some religious conservatives but some scientists had climbed on board the train of denial.

Blessed and burdened by a kind of naïve insistence, I asked why. There must be reasons for this apathy, right? And better to be naïve, it seemed, than to make arrogant assumptions. Better to be so than to simply plead to reason and compassion in what Swiss psychoanalyst Carl Jung called "fits of idealism" doomed to exhaust themselves and eventually peter out. Not that urgent protest is pointless, but it is not enough. What is needed—and here I believe Jung would agree with me—is to understand what is behind people's skepticism, apathy, and denial even in the face of factual evidence.

I suppose if I were more complacent and easygoing, or if I were not a therapist and intensely curious about what drives human behaviors, I might then have chosen a distraction or changed the subject, even if my concern continued internally. But that was not my way. My way was to toss and turn in frustration for a while and then decide to proceed on a kind of trip, so to speak—without the use of psychedelics, mind you, and without a clear map, either. My journey would be to explore the idea that just as there is a physical climate, so there is also a human climate, and that unless the human climate, at least on this side of the globe, became less adversarial, less hateful, less scared and scary, we would have little chance of saving the physical one.

I'll state one of my biases right here: While a few people I know think going backward into a simpler, more traditional world would be the best, I disagree. I see no practical sense in devolving, in pretending we can reject technology or relinquish the richness of human experience gleaned through what we call progress. There are also too many people in control of vast amounts of resources who would never consider giving up that power to retreat to the past. Instead—and here again, my developmental outlook is in play—I believe that our course through this personal and global crisis is forward, while we open our eyes to the darker side of progress, own what we see there, and address it.

I decided that on this trip I would both move about and stay still, noting what I saw and felt and learned. My intellect is more intuitive than scholarly, and I chose to trust this. Basically, I decided to value what I think of as my dancing mind, which tends to move in pretzel-like directions on its way toward a center, and use it as a travel resource, along with my knack for making human connections and my openness to reading and noticing.

I began to write, at first to document what I was experiencing. When doing so seemed pertinent or helpful,

I included things I already knew or had experienced previously. And so writing became a way for me to talk out loud, something I have seen—in therapy and in my own relationships—as a way of coming to new understandings. It was a way of clearing the atmosphere, clearing the cobwebs, and occasionally being surprised.

Surprise has been an element in this journey from the beginning. I observed early on how the apparently universal tendency to presume that our own assumptions about the way things are must be right relies, to some degree, on superstition. Going from superstition to surprise, then, became a goal of my inner travels, and it gradually became a guiding notion for the book that is here before you.

It was comforting to discover that I was not alone in this dancing approach to creativity. Theater director and choreographer Lee Sunday Evans is a family friend, so when she was featured in a *New York Times* article by Neil Genzlinger, I read it with enthusiasm.[1] I was taken aback (in a good way) to find that Evans's description of her directing style was similar to how I work—work as in doing therapy, writing, or thinking and feeling.

Genzlinger notes the frequent use of the term "leap of faith" in his conversation with Evans and playwright Kate Benson. In explaining how she couldn't explain the exact process of her work or what the product would look like to Benson, Evans said, "I came to it with this hunch that if I followed this thread about the movement, I could make it work, but I couldn't exactly promise her what it would look like or even explain it, because you can't really explain it till you see it." That rang true for me because, in my work with therapy clients especially, when I see or sense a thread of significance, I follow it even if I am not yet able to put it into words. I usually find that it leads gradually, through combinations of creativity and reasoning, toward a safer and fuller assessment of what is going on and where we are going.

In Evans's case, her play, once choreographed, quickly lost the uncertainty that surrounded its creative process. I'm afraid that is not the case with this writing. Early on, the writing started from a place of confusion and questioning and then moved to a place of more coherence. But then it changed. And then it changed again. And then it became clear that it would keep changing for a while. Gradually I understood that the book itself would be a process of peeling away layers of assumptions.

One example of this peeling away was discovering confirmation of my longstanding opinion that emotions hugely influence how we cooperate with or stay divided from each other at every level—individually, as families, in larger groups, and even globally.

Then, through months of writing and going through my own physical illness with its concomitant traumas, I came to realize that the context in which we live shapes how we feel emotions and even whether we know what we feel. So we can't very well talk about emotions unless we also consider whether the context—that is, the human climate—is working to guide and help or to repress and punish. The changes that both the book and I went through continued, thank the heavens, in the company of an editor who could help ground me as I attempted to find center even as I continued, and still continue, to dance away.

I offer here a series of chapters on the human climate, on the climates we face today. I can give only a partial view, of course, limited as I am by my own biases, superstitions, and traumas, even my own climates. But rather than letting that limitation cause me to retreat from this proposition, I chose to embrace it. I wanted once, as many others do, first to save my parents, then to save the world or, if not that, then make big changes for the good in this world. In fact, I can only do my best and let that settle where it does, without knowing beforehand what its effects will be.

The ride that is coming to and at you in the form of this book intends to bypass the usual brands of certainty and promises of a simple playbook. Life, as far as I'm concerned, is not supposed to be easy; it is supposed to be full. It is also supposed to be not so hard that it can't be managed. On this ride, you are signing up to allow me to talk to you out loud as I learn and share what I've discovered.

Having been asked once which shelf of the bookstore I envisioned this book to be on, I shirked and said a shelf would be a superfluous idea, since—like most authors—I wanted this to be a best seller and those don't have singular shelves. Then I said I didn't care and thought the question silly, though I also recognized that purveyors of books might want and even have to organize books by category.

My point really was that I mean to resist categories. These days, the desire to maintain categories—to be right, to win, to defeat—is rampant. The book is an attempt to talk about how to connect to ourselves and to others in a time of huge anxiety. Such a topic and such times demand that we question categories, if not break through them.

I can be as defiant as the next person. When people commit injustices that seem egregious, I want to scream to make them stop. When there is a war that seems unfair and corrupt, I want to march against it. And when people stubbornly insist on their position even in the face of evidence to the contrary, I want to convince them that they are wrong. And yet . . . and yet, I know better. I know it's pointless for me to lecture; it never worked for me, that is for sure. If I'm lectured to, I lose interest and say "whatever." So I understand.

Another thing is for sure. I've learned on my journey that a great deal of what is important to learn lies not only in talking out loud but also in the spaces beneath and between the words. I am hopeful that the coming chapters allow you enough space to breathe in your own thoughts and fancies and questions. I have little doubt that, if allowed that space, you will find you have more to add to what I say, and so your additions can be a viable beginning to the formation of different kinds of community. Many people are exhausted, depleted, lonely, and self-conscious or ashamed of that loneliness. And while no new religion is to be found here, this book does suggest that asking questions and sharing our doubts and feelings with each other can help us grow and thus feel safer in the world and within ourselves.

Lastly, in the chapters that follow, I am aware that my role—as cotraveler but also guide—can be one that delivers disappointment. There are books that promise it all: the youthful look, the perfect digestion, peace from morning till night, and of course money. What I can promise is honesty—as much as I can muster—and, I dare say, an interesting if imperfect journey.

So here is to the adventure that follows. Here is to curiosity. And here's to our being and feeling in safe—certainly safe enough—company.

1

A Human Climate

When I began what I think of as my personal course of study about why things haven't been going so well for us humans despite our having so much knowledge at our disposal, I knew this would be mostly an experiential inquiry. Not only am I not equipped by training or temperament to do hard research; I had not seen much discussion of the underlying dynamics perpetuating climate change denial—along with famine, genocide, and gross economic inequalities, not to mention constant wars and threats of wars. In other words, my driving question about *why* these issues not only haunt us but are evidently worsening wasn't taking up media space on anything like a daily basis.

The background I brought to this exploration also factored into my experiential approach. My years as a social worker, helping individuals and families deal with issues such as unwanted pregnancies, foster care, and abusive situations in poor and multiproblem families furthered my natural proclivity toward prioritizing people's experiences over what I saw as a colder and more analytical view of social problems. Similarly, my firsthand knowledge of psychotherapy as both a therapist and a client led me to mistrust much of what is conventional in the therapy field—for instance, techniques discussed in manuals and how-to books. Over the years, I came to trust instead the layers of feeling, conflict, and also clarity that emerge during the interactive process between therapist and client. This experiential approach informs my understanding of the topic at hand, which, like my impressionistic research into it, is very much a work in progress.

As I explained in the introduction, when it struck me that the atmosphere inside people as well as between and among them is what needs drastic attention, I summoned up—without much planning—the notion that there exists a social and psychological climate, not only a physical one. That climate quickly became, in my mind, a *human* climate, having various features as well as many problems to consider.

I have come to see the human climate as the social and emotional context in which we relate to each other. It is the repository of assumptions and standards in which we discuss and resolve issues, deny them, or use them to make war and do harm. While I speak of a single human climate, there are actually many, perhaps countless, such climates. Just as there are multiple physical microclimates around the world, so there are different human microclimates in different places, for different people, or at different times for the same people. Every human grouping—from couples to families to companies to nations—seems to have a climate. This includes the office, the university, Congress, and much more. A human climate may provide a context for growth or its opposite, for resolving problems or the opposite, and so on. It comprises the atmosphere and, importantly, the mood.

~

To illustrate how a human climate can be complex, sometimes paralyzing, and how freeing up the climate can help, I'd like to tell you about a particular family that came to see me. Jonathan, the ten-year-old son, was periodically threatening to kill his two younger sisters in their sleep and was throwing things at his parents and sisters when he got frustrated. Neither parents nor siblings seemed too alarmed by this, saying they were pretty much "used to it." Still, the climate in the home was always tense, mostly about Jonathan's tantrums. While the two girls were tamer in terms of temperament, Jonathan was very active and easily frustrated. His parents hated to see him suffer, so they gave in to his demands for a later bedtime, for more ice cream, and so on. However, not infrequently they raged at him, called him "impossible" and "spoiled," and put him to bed without dinner.

The unpredictability of the family climate's rules was producing a boy who was becoming a tyrant, and an unhappy one at that. Yes, he was easily frustrated. But what he needed were parents who could set limits that were also good for him and who could tolerate his expressions of frustration without defaulting to pacifying him or giving in to his demands. He needed to feel that his emotions could be tolerated, that things would be okay after a bit of time, instead of being either blamed or placated—comfort and consolation being different from shutting someone up by giving in only.

For the climate to change for the better, the parents would have to stop blaming Jonathan for his inconsistent behavior and become accountable for their own inconsistencies. However, since his aggressive patterns had already developed, this shift would not be easy. I spent several sessions with the parents, helping them deal with their own conflicts and build agreements between them; for example, if Jonathan had a temper tantrum, one of them would take him to another room and offer to sit out the upset with him. It was important for them to know, together, what they would do if his behavior escalated to the next level—whether they would sit down with him to talk or take him in for a therapy session if nothing else seemed to be working.

In one therapy session we actually talked with Jonathan about placing him in a treatment center if necessary for the well-being of everyone in the family, including him. This was said in front of him not as an idle threat but out of genuine concern for safety in the home. And the parents needed to be ready, with help, to carry through on this if necessary. The rules and structures of a constructive climate require consequences so they have meaning, and those setting the limits have to be prepared for their not always being received with agreement or delight.

None of us knew how violent Jonathan might become when faced with such firm limits on his behavior, and we had to face the fact that he might become seriously aggressive. We met a few times a week for a while, usually with both Jonathan and his parents. Jonathan was able to articulate, with help, that he felt bad for being treated differently. He hated his sisters for being "the lucky ones," he said, but he was mostly angry at his parents, who were so often upset with him. He described them as "changing their minds all the time." As Jonathan was able to feel heard, his anger lessened. He was also able to express the sadness of feeling bad and being treated differently.

The therapy work also involved the two girls, who, in their own ways, were feeling left out of the special if conflictual bond between Jonathan and their parents. As family members shared pent-up emotions and perceptions and worked through them to the best point possible, tensions lessened. The climate became one of greater relaxation, which allowed the family members to talk to each other rather than simply explode in reaction. One could say the relaxation became contagious, which was something everyone wanted and needed.

When there is enough relaxation as well as structure in a climate, people tend to feel safer. Conflicts and changes can be confronted without permanently jeopardizing someone's sense of esteem or belonging. Safety comes most naturally in a climate where the full range of feelings is accepted.

~ ⁀

When a family climate is sensitive to the needs of both children and parents, there can be room for the children to learn the hard but important truth that disappointments happen as part of life. Optimally, this allows for what I call "the gift of disappointment." We see many adults among us—too many, and in high places, as well—who are overly empowered to feel and act as if they can have or do anything they like. The ideal corrective is to have had a period in childhood when they were stood up to and shown the limits of power of any of us.

Limits and boundaries are crucial in childhood—they wind up making the child feel safe, if they are communicated without shaming or a punitive attitude. However, it can be both difficult and counterintuitive for a parent to get through this part of his or her child's growing because it involves the parent's being the agent of disappointment. "It rained, so I couldn't get to the store." "I'm sorry. I get it that you want to stay up all night, but you're overtired and knocking into walls, and it needs to be time for bed." "Your siblings are going to stay here, at home with us, even though you just said you wished they would go away for good." This may seem simple enough, but watch the face of a young child when the disappointment is present-ed; the child can feel betrayed, having begun life feeling he or she is powerful enough to call the parent on command and have his or her needs met. But as the child's brain develops, he or she becomes more aware and then discovers that complete power is actually nonexistent. In the best of scenarios, the adult looks the child in the eye, as it were, and says, "Yes, it's true, I can't deliver everything you'd like, and what's more, we'll have to sit through this pain you're feeling without pacifying it with a bunch of cookies." Okay, maybe one cookie, but there is no getting around the child's sadness and deflation at learning that the parent is not perfect and the child is neither empowered nor entitled to access perfection.

For the child, this discovery is nothing less than tragic, or at least it feels this way. It's a disruption in the parent-child relationship. The optimal consolation I see is that the preceding stage of the relationship, in which "My wish is your command" held sway, had trust and honesty at its center. For then it has the best chance of evolving into a relationship of "We'll get through this together," which is foundational for the more complex relationships of adulthood. This stage, coming for different children at different points of development and different ages, also encourages socialization outside the home. The child realizes, in other words, that sitting at home and insisting on having magical powers won't result in all one's needs being met all the time.

Many parents want to keep meeting all the needs of their child and find it inconceivable to be the agent of this level of disappointment. They keep giving their children tons of stuff and never say no. We know this scenario as engendering a child we think of as spoiled. The label "spoiled" never sounded fair to me because it seems to put the blame squarely on a child, who, to my mind, is a victim of a parent's own anxiety and avoidance in this realm. After all, the parent who never says no can feel better about himself or herself, at least temporarily.

The other side of the coin of being the ever-giving, always "good" parent is being the blamer. I'm referring here to using disappointment as a punishment or as a decree of wrongdoing—for example, "I wouldn't have hit you if you hadn't made me so mad." It's still a way of trying to be immune to the child's disappointment, the illusion being that "I'm only setting this limit or creating disappointment because I'm being held hostage by this terrible child."

The downside of limit-setting by blaming is that the person on the receiving end feels bad not only in the moment but for a long time after. If a child is taught that every limit or disappointment comes with blame and shaming, then every disappointment in life needs to be blamed on someone. The target of blame can wind up being ourselves, whether individually or collectively, or people we designate as "other." Whoever is the recipient, to rely on blame is a way of not integrating disappointment—at times fixable, at times inevitable—as part of life.

In certain respects, a therapist is also an agent of disappointment. Most people in therapy want a re-do of life and are disappointed when they realize the therapist can only be a witness, even a companion, but not the magical remaker of the past. (No judgment here; I know what it's like to yearn for starting all over again.)

Ultimately, the gift of disappointment is not just about a child's discovery that there are limits. It's about the mutuality of limits, as it touches on the loss of perfection and omnipotence for the parents as for the child and thus, by extension, for any of us. In some respects, disappointment is the loss of Eden. Yet when we unwrap the gift of disappointment, we are likely to find inside it the gem of increasing maturity that comes with increasing realism.

One of the most pressing problems we face in larger human climates—in institutions, towns, nations—is the search for absolute answers as opposed to settling into the realism of working together. Cooperation can be optimistic and even exciting, but it involves facing together real emotions, real pain, and real awareness of limitations. Being sober is not completely a somber proposition, but let's face it—it can't always compete with the drawing power of, for example, the hype of loud, adrenalin-fueled rallies and one person declaring the intention to "make America great again," or religions promising conquest of the world, with heaven for the faithful included.

As such, we and those who come after us are called upon to be growing up—not grown up entirely, since the growing never ends—so we can do our best to see what's going on as clearly as possible and to take action together as best we can to make needed change. The human and physical climates we live in require this from us.

2
Feelings as a Second Language

O ne of the first things I noticed as I began to explore the human climate was the extremes of divisiveness in the current sociopolitical climate, such that we almost take it for granted that leaders will be at each others' throats. Being a psychotherapist, I proposed and indeed sensed that this attraction to conflict and the apparently substantial difficulty in getting beyond it might have to do with divisions existing inside us, and that those internal disconnects are emotional in nature.

We never come to a situation without an attitude and temperament shaped by the history of our experiences—that is, without our emotions. Nor, it seems, are we helped much, in childhood or adulthood, in getting acquainted with our emotions, which range widely from rage to tenderness. Many of us are taught from scratch that it's not only not nice to act certain ways, it's also not nice to feel controversial feelings. This is a tough one because in various human microclimates, what is nice and what is naughty—or what is naughty but brave and applauded— can differ greatly.

Part of the issue is that too few of the people who guide us are themselves capable of embracing and containing a wide variety of feelings. If we have not been helped to own our feelings as children (we are told: "Don't cry," "Don't be a baby," "Don't be shy"), it can be hard for us to put them in a reasonably coherent perspective. We are moved to repress feelings that we aren't helped to name or that we perceive as nasty or unspeakable or unpleasant, pushing them deep inside us.

When we push feeling on top of feeling, they pile up, leading to a state of congestion. And when our emotional circulation is halted, it becomes harder and harder to think straight—for, as many of us know, feelings trump facts. They can cancel thinking entirely. When we don't realize that certain feelings exist in us, they can control us without our knowing.

I had already read up, and written up a bit as well, on the "shadow," a term coined by Swiss psychiatrist and psychoanalyst Carl Jung for the place in our unconscious where we hide any emotions considered too shameful or scary to acknowledge. From there, those emotions can do damage by exploding suddenly or being projected by us onto those whom we blame or fight, demean and demonize. We will visit this subject in more detail in chapter 7, but it feels important to say here that Jung's answer to the question "What do we do about our shadow?" has to do with our integrating our emotions. Most of us do not learn how to attend to our feelings so they can get along, as it were. Without some degree of emotional integration, it is hard to contain our emotions so they don't jump out and bite us or someone with whom we are trying to coexist.

In this sense, I see the optimal human climate as a kind of equal opportunity employer of emotions, by which I mean that emotions would be given the same respect as thoughts.

Because our emotions are to a great extent foreign to us and, as such, confusing, I have taken to considering them akin to a second language. Getting to know emotions better seems to me something like the study of a language, in that we can talk about feelings and how to contain their excesses and confusion just as we can talk about grammar and syntax. In becoming more fluent with feelings, we become more able to talk about their complexities—and vice versa.

Some feelings and memories can generate conflicts and controversy; even in the middle of a conversation meant to be constructive, things can go awry when one participant has a reaction that is emotional or triggers something emotional in the other. Even if both parties feel they have a grasp on their own emotions, one person may well have to translate the way he or she feels a particular feeling into the language of the listener. How else can we make sense to someone who thinks and feels differently?

By its nature, a language frames our perceptions. Just as in various languages there can be words for certain concepts that are not named or identified in others, so languages of emotion are likely to differ from person to person. So also, even if we become better equipped to know how we are feeling, we will still be called on to travel outside the language of our comfort zone, to understand—as a second language or perhaps a third or a fourth—the emotional context of people around us. In the process, we may also be prompted to reevaluate the certainty with which we may originally have approached the topic at hand.

It is often assumed that in an intimate relationship, a good partner will know, often anticipate, and at least try to satisfy the other person's emotional needs. It may be taken for granted that one partner will, in this way, complete the other. In fact, this is rarely the case. Rather, in relationships that have a bit of growing up in them, we try to know our own feelings enough to translate them for our partner, who has had different experiences. We also want to hear about the stories and meanings of the other person, setting aside the assumption that there is one truth, one emotional language, one way of seeing and feeling things.

This kind of exchange becomes more challenging with people whose emotional languages are very different from our own, even though they work and live close to us. A person who is politically liberal may argue with his or her conservative neighbors without being curious about their experience, their resentments, their perspective. Instead, the liberal neighbor may impose his or her own emotional language as primary, assuming that it contains the only explanations and values worth owning. If the neighbors do not establish a common language of curiosity and exchange, the divisions between them become reinforced, not reduced.

The value of learning another's language came up for me as I learned more about the Islamic practice of women wearing the veil. Growing up and living with the cultural language of the West, I viewed the veil a sign of subservience and thus a message of disempowerment to the women. That language was challenged and then expanded when I learned that for many women who wear the veil, it is a sign of dignity, while the Western practice of including nearly naked or seductively dressed women in advertising appears to them as an insult to women.

We think, therefore we are. But our thinking is either enhanced or compromised by how aware we are of our emotional language and prejudices. When we are reasonably comfortable with our own emotions, we feel more secure. We tend to feel less threatened, and so we are less likely to insist that our way of seeing or feeling is the only way.

Ideally, we learn the language of our emotions as we grow up. For an infant, feelings can be overwhelming and even chaotic. A baby can be crying because he or she is hungry and tired and needs a diaper changed and is in need of comforting, all at the same time.

Part of the parent's role is learning the baby's emotional language and language style, something that comes mostly through trial and error. This involves being willing to be confused, to not yet understand but nevertheless offer comfort, which communicates safety and recognition to the baby. The parent comes to know the differences between a hungry cry, a sleepy cry, a need-for-affection cry, and an urgency cry so he or she can respond more specifically. This helps the infant feel that the parent is reliable and that the infant's ability to feel and to communicate is reliable, as well. The baby becomes increasingly comfortable with the language of emotions, even without yet having words.

As the infant grows into a child, the parent conceptualizes the feelings the child expresses and provides verbal language for them, helping the child identify feelings and make sense of them. Even to recognize "I am tired" takes a certain level of maturation and learning. When children are allowed to express a variety of emotions without being punished for them while learning to identify them, they begin to manage many of their feelings themselves with less anxiety. This happens especially when the adults allow nuances of feeling to be communicated and don't insist on their own script.

On the other hand, if infants and children are left alone with their emotions or are shamed or ignored when they do express them, they learn to try to bury them or deny them. But since feelings cannot just go away, they remain part of the child's psychic anatomy, piled on top of each other, as it were, jumbled, unprocessed—that is, congested.

How can congested emotions get unstuck? Often, the place to begin is with whatever emotion is showing up. Like starting to unravel a tangle of string by reaching for the first loose end that presents itself, we can follow the thread of consecutive emotions as they present themselves. Sometimes, not infrequently, the emotion that shows up is resistance to feeling a feeling, so it can be important, for instance in a therapeutic context, to start with why expressing feelings is, or was, scary or even unwise. The last thing we want to do is to lead someone into real or felt danger of humiliation or other harm should that person express something taboo or explosive.

As emotions become less congested, they can become more fluid. When they become more fluid, there begins to be some space around them so we can start to recognize them and to recognize one from another. Our comfort with our feelings increases. Moving in and out of strong feelings, we gradually realize that even a strong feeling is not permanent and that it may not be as scary as initially perceived. Furthermore, when strong emotions are met with comfort and calming, emotional integration and regulation can hopefully begin. In this way we don't have to remain a victim of our feelings or end discussions—or relationships, even—when strong emotions do come up.

Of course, we can expect to stumble and fall along the way. In trying to regulate our emotions, we have to regulate (at least acknowledge, as a start) our tendencies to judge some emotions harshly, since otherwise we remain stymied. It all takes a lot of practice. Hopefully, we have supports to help us coming from what we read and hear, and from people who can remind us of the humanity of all emotions.

When we get to know our feelings better, we begin to read them as signals, as information about our internal state in response to conditions both within and around us. Sometimes a strong feeling is a warning of danger, alerting us to take appropriate action. For instance, when we are frightened, we can look around, both inside and out, to see what is triggering that fear, or we can ask for help in figuring it out. Fear isn't always bad; in fact, it can help us plan how to make things better or how to adapt to a difficult circumstance. This kind of fear is termed "signal anxiety." You *should* become afraid, for instance, if you're walking in the woods and a bear crosses your path. When we're not emotionally congested, we can trust fear as a signal and strategize or act based on it. But if it's constant, it becomes a backdrop coloring everything we see and feel.

Though we can become better acquainted with the language of emotions, it's unrealistic to expect complete fluency. Fluency in any language, even the one we grew up speaking, is relative. Languages also change over time, as do we. Someone else may describe a feeling we are not that familiar with or don't have as yet in our vocabulary of experienced emotions. There can be a certain humility about this experience, since it means acknowledging that we do not and cannot know everything, even about ourselves and our capacity to feel.

Emotional fluency doesn't mean that our feelings become completely predictable or we can comfortably manage them all the time. They will at times take us by surprise and even take us over, overwhelm us. This is simply the nature of emotions. Part of fluency may well be our awareness during or after (so often it is after) the experience of "losing it" in one fashion or another.

⌒ͻ

Certainly, describing feelings after the fact can be oh-so-different from being in their midst. The words we use to speak of feelings are hopefully connected with those feelings, but sometimes words about emotions are used in a way that distances us from the emotions. Words can be used to define feelings quickly and glibly while masking the emotions themselves, which may be complex and chaotic. Here is where I have found it helpful to talk about ceilings and basements.

The ceilings, to my mind, are the places of neat, organized language used to name emotions, while the basements are where the emotions themselves, in their more raw forms, reside. (I speak of them in the plural, since they vary and are different for everyone, also because an individual has more than one.) Basements are where we can get in touch with the real messiness of emotions, which is sometimes crucial, for instance, in moments of grief or trauma—or intense passion, for that matter. Having reasonable supplies of emotional fluidity and fluency means you are more ready and able to descend into the basements, have a fight for a few minutes, and come back up.

Some of us have triggers that push us into what feels more like a dungeon than a basement. That space needs exploring too, since otherwise some feelings will be forever condemned. But that also takes practice—tons and tons.

Some therapies and therapists try to deal with emotions from the ceilings only, teaching the client formulas with which to talk about what he or she is feeling while hovering above and thus out of touch with the emotions themselves. Such scripts induce us to fake emotional fluency while our messier states remain underground, where havoc can reign.

I worked with Andy, a young man in his twenties who had serious drug problems. He wanted to stop using drugs, but that was only on some days, and besides, he was surrounded by a group of friends who all partook. I offered Andy an open climate, in that I saw him for therapy whether he was high or not in the hope that he would feel enough support to reach out when he was readier to commit to treating the addiction. When he had developed enough trust to do some serious work on his addiction, we agreed that he needed a better container than the frequent outpatient therapy sessions he was having with me, so he was admitted to a prestigious and supposedly excellent rehab center, one his parents were willing and able to pay for.

After Andy had been in rehab a couple of weeks, he had down pat the so-called language of feelings he was being taught. The acceptable sentence structure went like this: "When you (or he, she, they, I) do such and such, it makes me think this. And when I think this, I feel that." The assumption underlying this approach was that we think before we feel—something I am not at all sure about. Perhaps we *assume* before we feel sometimes, but I heartily doubt we really think before we feel.

In any case, the program identified four acceptable feelings to choose from: anger, fear, rage, and love—hardly an imaginative variety. Ouch, this was a hard one. It implied that it is possible to fly up to the ceilings to define what are complex, intense, and often confusing and conflicted emotions with a single word—and a noun, to top it off. I do realize that when a person is in a chaotic state, simplified language can be organizing. But when it is used to control emotions and their expression, it becomes a subtle form of bullying.

Initially, the rehab center staff wanted me to collaborate with them in Andy's therapy. But in the first month, they realized my basements-oriented approach was so different from their ceilings-only approach that they encouraged Andy to see his connection with me as destructive, and they allowed us to communicate only in the presence of one of their staff members. In one conversation with Andy and a staff member, I was asked to use their institutional language, so I tried. I said something like, "When you told me you were planning to use drugs at home, I thought you would. And then I felt worried." I paused and asked the staff member if it was permissible to use the word "worried" for a feeling. She said yes, though I'm not sure if she got my sarcasm.

In his earlier therapy sessions with me, Andy had allowed me to see much of what was in his basement, including a lot of shame internalized from dealings with his authoritarian and disapproving parents. Now, in this institutional setting, he was lured into going along with their program, partly because they seemed so smooth and certain. They minimized the messier sides of him, his mixed feelings, and gave him a formula that made him feel better than the person he "used to be." As such, he felt he was better than me as well, since I had been the one to dignify the messier parts of him that he was now rejecting.

When Andy finally got out of the program, he made an appointment to see me, during which he apologized for turning against me and said, "You know, that place was really a cult." He had been lonely, he said, and he had missed our way of working—missed having someone with him in the basements who let him talk about what was there. It was only when he recognized his lack of comfort with making believe he was on top of things that he became aware that something was off. Only then could he begin to interrupt his distancing from his basement and pursue a treatment program that would include all the parts of him.

While Andy was able to choose for himself a basements approach over a ceilings approach, a couple I worked with, Jules and Marisa, were suffering because they had no idea the basements existed. In one of their early sessions, Jules and Marisa seemed particularly eager to tell me how aware of their emotions they were and how well they were doing. It seemed to me a little excessive, influenced perhaps by a need to please. When I pointed this out as a possibility, they wanted to explore it.

Both of them talked about the humiliation they had felt from therapists in their several previous tries at couples' therapy when they revealed the ugliness of some of their scenes of mutual loss of control. Marisa had thrown full cups of coffee at Jules, and he had kicked in one wall in their apartment so many times that they needed to call someone to rebuild it. One therapist had told them they obviously weren't capable of doing "real" therapy and were "clearly too immature to be married." His comments made them feel so uncomfortable that they wanted to leave, but they also told me they thought his assessment was right. They felt ashamed of their raging behavior. They hoped to find someone who could help them cover it over and "just calm down."

In fact, they wanted to be honest about their emotions but didn't know how. What was stopping them was their fear of being humiliated if they exposed their real feelings. Thus they had been all too willing to accept a language of good behavior, which in the moment promised a simple and possibly forever solution.

When I introduced the idea of ceilings and basements and said that so often advice comes from the ceilings while people are living in the basements, both of them smiled, and Marisa said she felt relieved. The concept offered them a way of reframing their perceptions, and it gave respect to their emotions, which was essential in order for us to explore those emotions and their triggers.

Jules and Marisa's story, among others, drove home to me just how easily the therapy climate can echo the humiliation people have experienced elsewhere about their deeper emotions. A kind of insult occurs when you're in the basement and someone talks to you from the ceiling. It can cause more shame, so you do not feel free to react honestly to that insult. It can also evoke early feelings of vulnerability, of again being the child facing the big person who seems so sure. The humiliation leads to becoming more closed off, hiding more, and experiencing increased self-loathing. Just as the worst part of depression can be being depressed about being depressed, the worst part of humiliation can be being or feeling humiliated for feeling humiliated in the first place.

Congestion doesn't always clear up that simply, of course. Sometimes people remain tense; the emotional knots don't release so easily. And when we get stuck enough in emotional congestion and stuck in fighting each other and our own uncomfortable feelings, we can come to believe that this is the only way to live. We can be seduced into thinking that excitement is found only in destroying.

None of this is to say that once we get our emotions better sorted out and are relatively fluent in them, everything will be okay and we'll live happily every after. We can still be pushed into emotional states, and out of them, by the human climate where we find ourselves. And while we can influence the emotional climate around us, we cannot control it. Trauma, past and present, internal and external, exposes us to serious vulnerabilities and even fragilities in the arena of feelings. When the human climate is such that an important arena like emotions is not discussed or is discussed only from the ceilings, we can expect to find learning the language of feelings will be both challenging and choppy.

We can be only so fluent. There are always emotions or nuances or combinations of emotions we've not yet felt. The best of us can become emotionally tongue-tied when attacked. Part of being fluent, then, is holding realistic expectations about ourselves and being ready to make mistakes. Being able to interrupt ourselves in the midst of strong and sometimes sudden emotions can be a goal, even if one that is not easily reached. This kind of interruption, often while adrenalin is in full force, takes practice. Expectations can shift and we can mature, but man, this is a rough one. Even so, learning the language of emotions, which so strongly influences how we think, is one of the tasks desperately needing our attention.

3
Talking Out Loud

I am a terrible debater, and I have witnesses to prove it. To me, a debate sounds like verbal bullets fired rapidly to destroy an opponent. However, some people are great at debating, and one of my friends not only is superior at it but loves the thrill of it. He also enjoys verbally throwing out his thoughts as if into the air and seeing what comes back to him. In other words, he can play devil's advocate, though he does not try so much to prove the other person wrong as to better understand his own views on a given subject.

Throwing thoughts out there in order to sort things out is close to what I call "talking out loud." Talking out loud can be the combination of babble, ranting, and occasional brilliance verbalized by a therapy patient who is free-associating. In the therapy room, whichever role I'm in (patient or therapist), free-associating is one of my favorite elements. No particular agenda, no summary of daily or weekly events or symptoms is required. It can be simply reporting how the mind and the emotions are going—except when fear or other strong emotions overwhelm the chance of speaking more slowly, at which point the intense emotion itself must become the focus. But there will be time for slower speaking again, once the feelings get easier and safer.

Talking out loud, as meant here, is exposing one's thoughts so as to reevaluate one's own position and also let that position be influenced by the responses of another—a listener or listeners. It implies an invitation not to keep one's thoughts secret due to fear of retribution or being cast aside, and to share without any motive to manipulate. Talking out loud offers an opportunity to shift understandings and to find ways to collaborate constructively.

To talk out loud in this sense, there has to be a modicum of safety. This is because talking out loud in this way requires a climate where one can be comfortable sounding ignorant as well as wise, prejudiced as well as open, where one can change one's mind and be surprised to hear oneself voicing an idea that had been elusive or appeared obnoxious five minutes before.

Talking out loud as I mean it is definitely not talking belligerently or shutting up other people with intimidation. Although it can be loud, even protesting, it doesn't have to be so. It can be quiet, even a whisper, since words do not have to be loud in volume to be important. Talking out

loud is also starkly different from the super-speed conversations that have become normal today and from the
defensive posturing we default to when we feel threatened.
If we feel pressured to prove our point at any price, we
may well not have the ease needed to see a contradiction
in our own argument and thinking.

Talking out loud to another person is certainly not
always the stuff of ease or romance. We may become
anxious before the conversation because we can't anticipate what the other person is going to say, or because
we anticipate the person's saying something critical. On
the other hand, talking with certain people at certain
times—when the climate is relaxed, for example—can be
very freeing, even lighthearted, silly, or wickedly funny. We
may feel known; we may come to a solution that works for
all parties involved. Even when there is conflict, talking
out loud can be a way of decongesting tangled and stuffed
emotions, or at least bringing to light what is getting in the
way of resolution.

The words "out loud" suggest this is always a process
involving another person, someone to listen and be a
sounding board. But I find that talking out loud can also be
internal, a way to process what's on the inside. When the
climate inside ourselves is relaxed enough, we can simply
let ideas sit for a while, let them mature. The internal ease
may allow a change of heart, of mind, or allow questions
that hadn't been clear or evident before.

For me, talking out loud is a pivotal concept with
regard to the human climate, since it involves sharing,

pondering, developing feelings and ideas in an atmosphere open enough to allow the exchange and change of ideas. It is a way of speaking that allows something genuine to happen within a conversation. It is accompanied by a willingness to pause, to be questioned—perhaps even be contradicted by the listener or oneself. There is space to say, "Wait a minute, I just said being in a church gives me the creeps, but I also remember an experience in a church some months ago when I was so moved that I was crying," or, "I think Starbucks is for white hipsters and it has terrible coffee, but I realize I love the one in my neighborhood." We're so used to having to prove our perspective or follow a set of norms that saying "I'm confused" doesn't always win a lot of points. However, confusion, for all its discomfort, can be a priceless step on the way to genuine curiosity, to finding out something new, and perhaps even to collaboration.

In psychotherapy, one aspect of helping the client get to deeper self-awareness comes through the therapist's invitation to the client to talk out loud. This is a complicated invite, however. People who come for therapy do not typically shift instantly from being shut down to opening up like a leaky faucet, certainly not on command. On the other hand, some people, those whose impulses are running away with them, may be all too willing to speak and cannot stop. So also, the therapist has to be ready to listen to the expression of deep and chaotic feelings, resistances, and possibly controversial thoughts and feelings with seriousness and respect. This is not always easy. Sometimes a client can be quite prejudiced against talking out loud or can fear, consciously or unconsciously, revealing and thus having to acknowledge unexpected emotion.

Eric was in his thirties when he came to see me. His father had had a heart attack and heart surgery two months earlier, and Eric hadn't seen his father since the operation. He wanted to visit but felt like he couldn't. Something was stopping him from dialing the number to make a date. His father was a Jewish rabbi and was quite scholarly. The climate in the family was competitive, expressed mostly in conversations that were more like debates and always had a winner and a loser. Eric was different, he told me during his first session. He didn't feel made from the same family cloth. Even though he was very successful as a landscape photographer, he wasn't good at public speaking, and even when speaking privately to people, he usually felt clumsy and floundering. When we talked of his dad, he said his father was a "real intellectual" who could solve just about anything through reasoning. I asked Eric how that made him feel about his seeking out therapy, and he said "weak." It seemed that Eric felt both angry and inferior in his father's presence.

What wound up happening is kind of a long story, but as Eric rambled and meandered during his sessions, it became clear to both of us that he very much enjoyed talking and in fact was rather good at it. He was able to pause one day and look up at me to say, "You know, I'm really not half bad at this. Maybe it's all of them who can't talk and me who is okay." It was a joke, but it had some seriousness in it. Eric was more articulate than he had been made out to be, and in becoming more aware of this in therapy, he felt that he wanted to—and also that he could—reach out to his father.

Eric asked if I'd consider doing a few joint sessions with him and his father, and I said sure. It turned out that his father had quite a good sense of humor. During the first session, after he told me repeatedly that he didn't see himself as judgmental when he looked in the mirror, I asked him if he had ever considered buying another mirror, to which he laughed. Eric was able to say he was realizing he was smarter than he had thought, and his dad said, "Well, I knew that." His father was arrogant but not unreachable, and he was not uninterested, either. It turned out that they could start to talk—out loud—even while Eric found he needed to bring the discussion back to a conversational tone when his dad took to debating with him.

The capacity to talk out loud can be crucial with young children who have lost trust in their capacity to communicate and in the adults around them wanting to listen. These children can get tagged as nonverbal when the real issue is that they associate verbalizing with trouble or fear.

Rachel was five when I began to work with her and her mother. The referral came from a law guardian and had to do with legal decisions about her visitations with her father. In the first few sessions, Rachel was speechless, quiet, with a scared look in her eyes. My sense was that Rachel had been put on the spot for too long and too often. She had, in essence, been cross-examined by lawyers and forensic psychologists. What made it worse was that the lawyers and therapists were very much seduced to side with her father, who could be charming even though his charm rather turned on and off in an instant.

In the sessions with Rachel and her mother, I did therapy with Rachel indirectly; any pushing her into direct expression needed to go by the wayside. I gave her some play materials and began talking with her mother. I didn't know if Rachel would join in, but this way she had a direct experience of a safer climate—not by my telling her it was safe to say anything but by my proving it to her. She heard my directness in speaking with her mother even as her mother and I got along. With all the tension between her parents, if I had been another person attacking her mother, she would not have trusted me.

As often happens, not only was Rachel curious about my conversations with her mom, but she grew excited and began interrupting us with questions or volunteering her own perceptions. After some months of these sessions, she began asking to speak to me on her own, usually for only moments at a time. When we finally did meet with her father in the room, she would whisper to me her thoughts if it felt too risky to express them out loud in front of him. Interestingly, as her trust increased, she would let me know when I could verbalize to him what she had just said to me. And even though that wouldn't get a positive response from him, Rachel still seemed sturdier internally because she had an ally at her side. She also seemed much more fluent on an emotional level in general. As she found her fire, she became spunky, even playful. She became a contender in her own life.

~∘

A necessary companion to talking out loud in the manner I am discussing is listening. In other words, if someone is talking out loud, is someone else present who is willing to hear what is being said? And not just hear it but also be affected by it—that is, listen actively? It is not always easy to listen in a way that allows what someone is saying to have an effect, because it means that we who are listening may have to shift. We may have to change an opinion or see things differently or start to cry because we are upset. However, changing our minds when they have been set in stone is something we have to contend with if we want to move forward—that is, evolve.

One of my favorite examples of the power of talking out loud is the Hans Christian Andersen fairy tale "The Emperor's New Clothes." In the story, two weavers appear at the emperor's court to promise him a new set of magnificent clothes. They tell him the clothing will not be visible to people who are incompetent or stupid. An announcement is made that only those of superior mind will see the robes the emperor wears as he is paraded through the town, so his subjects, not wanting to appear stupid, ooh and aah in admiration as the emperor passes by. However, a boy who is watching the parade with his mother is oblivious to the import of the announcement, so he speaks his mind, saying out loud, "But the emperor is naked; he has no clothes on at all." One by one, the townspeople and then the emperor's cronies change gears. Responding to the contagion of the truth, they begin declaring their authentic perceptions—that the king is naked—out loud. The weavers are run out of town, and common sense reigns again—for how long, we are not told.

This tale makes several points. It illustrates how, under pressure to conform, people can make an unspoken agreement to not see what is right in front of them. Also, while in some climates the revelation of new information correcting a false belief evokes ridicule or punishment of the speaker, this does not happen here. This suggests that the climate of the empire is flexible, not authoritarian—that the "news," even if previously denied, is not denied insistently. We also see that the climate between the boy and his mother is flexible; she does not shame him for saying what he notices.

The story, of course, describes how gullible the emperor and the rest of the crowd—the rest of us—can be. We can notice only what we're told to notice. If we are told that our leader is the greatest and this message is repeated through imagery and song, poetry and law, we may, as in some countries and religions, not dare to question the fallibilities of that leader or even the notion that there is only one true leader or only one set of truths.

This story also interrupts our assumptions about hierarchy. The mother let her son teach her and the other adults; she let him be smarter than her. Though a child, he was the one who challenged the established hierarchy of power. Even if this does not happen often enough in real life, stories and fairy tales often remind us of the wisdom of listening to the talking out loud of those we don't expect to be wise, especially when what they say has the unquestionable ring of truth.

~∂

One of the reasons for the rampant divisiveness currently on the US national stage may be the absence of openness in the national climate to talking out loud and to listening. Where the mood is ruled by insult, truth-telling by an adult (not to mention a child) is likely to be dismissed, turned into hype, or called false news. But this doesn't mean we can't begin to talk out loud anyway about the mood of our body politic. I got to explore this point when I did an interview with Robin DiAngelo, a white antiracist, for a *Huffington Post* blog.[2]

DiAngelo talked about "white fragility" in relation to racism. She pointed out that because white people, especially liberal whites, see themselves as good people (as most people tend to do) and see racism as bad, they assume they are not racist. For this reason, she suggests, liberal whites rarely consider their complicity in racism in the form of white privilege. Thus, when accused of being racist, they shut down and won't talk about it, which contributes to the perpetuation of racism in the culture at large.

Identifying as a white liberal myself, I found myself feeling quite defensive on hearing this. Then I realized my reaction was exactly what DiAngelo was talking about, which shook me out of my defensiveness and into talking and listening further. There was an opening in the conversation, and since I knew her purpose was not to criticize and certainly not to humiliate, I asked what she thought the solution was to white fragility. She said the first step is to find ways to talk about it, and here I might add "out loud." She added that if we're not doing our part to talk about it and make it a subject that receives the attention it needs, we are merely contributing to racism.

While talking out loud is crucial, it can sometimes be equally important simply to sit with feelings and thoughts, to reflect, and to refrain from speaking. A client of mine described his stepmother as a lovely person but one who "leaves no space to think things through. She has no concept that some silences do not have to be interrupted."

Even in therapy, sometimes the client needs help in being quiet—at points, one could say, even shutting up. When a young woman, in a session with her mother, berated her mother for neglecting her and causing her lifelong suffering again and again until it began to seem endless, I was able to say to her, "Listen, do you think you could keep some of this to yourself?" I had known her long enough and we had a solid enough relationship that I could say this. I was trying to help her put a lid on her tendency to barrage her mother without allowing space for feelings and thoughts to settle some and for her mother to respond. Talking out loud means the opposite of endless iterations. It has more to do with allowing room to breathe in real emotion and allowing the evolution of awareness as well.

Clearly, on personal and more global levels, the idea of talking out loud needs more than a little work. The first step may well be to talk out loud about talking out loud. This is because, well, dammit, it is hard. It requires interest and some safety, curiosity, and willingness not to degrade or be degraded. It can also be surprising, since when we aren't operating on automatic pilot, we can actually be surprised, even by our own thoughts and feelings. We may find that we like people we thought we only hated, and we may discover other viewpoints besides the ones we tend to hold all too often.

4

Across the Developmental Divide

As I explored the realm of the human climate further, my question "*Why* are we so stuck in divisiveness instead of applying the wisdom we have to make the changes that need making?" morphed into the question "*How* did we get here?" This shift was only natural, given my bias toward a developmental approach not only in therapy but also in other matters. I saw that we got here partly because of how we—all of us, from all socioeconomic levels and walks of life—grew up—specifically, whether in our earliest years we were nurtured strictly with a developmental approach or a behavioral approach.

According to *Merriam-Webster's Collegiate Dictionary* (11th ed.), the term "developmental" comes from "develop," which means to "go through a process of natural growth, differentiation, or evolution by successive changes." The word connotes a gradual evolution or unfolding, and because of the gradualness, an increase of depth and stability. In childrearing and child development, the developmental approach emphasizes the process more than the achievements, whereas the behavioral approach tends to see growth in terms of milestones achieved while minimizing the effects of the tactics taken to reach them.

The trouble with the behavioral approach is that while punishment and even humiliation of a child—by a parent, let's say—may result in the child's behaving the way the parent requires at that moment, the child can experience this kind of treatment traumatically. A tension, even a disconnect, is created between the surface behavioral adaptation and the authentic feelings hidden underneath. That internal disconnect then tends to breed divisions between ourselves and the world outside ourselves.

In some cases, even professionals can go as far as to ignore a child's truth and developmental needs. A certain forensic psychologist whom I know was hired to sort out the parental visiting arrangements of a divorced couple. Both of their two young boys were reluctant to be with their father for long, as he spent most of his time drinking or watching television, though occasionally he was quite charming to people of his choosing. The psychologist was bent on insisting on the father's rights (fathers' rights being his main professional interest), so he went about finding methods to enforce weekend visitations. Everyone drinks sometimes, and everyone watches television, he argued, and the boys are probably exaggerating in their description of their father's behavior. He went on to blame the mother for her sons' apprehensions, and he told her this (he repeated it to me with no compunction whatsoever): "Children are puppies. You can get them to do anything you want."

The tactics of this psychologist were obnoxious, to say the least. They exemplify the astonishing coldness of someone who wants a particular behavioral result now at any price and will present himself convincingly as the unquestionable authority to achieve it, oblivious to whether the outcome is harmful or good for the children, and even the adults, involved.

~⌒ঌ

Parents (as well as friends, helping professionals, teachers, and others who work with children) who adopt a developmental approach to raising children tend to bring empathy and mutuality into the process. For example, a parent might comfort a small child who is shy without predicting that the shyness is making a lasting imprint on the child. That is, the parent sees that growing up is gradual. Social awkwardness is usually grown out of. The context for much of the comforting, aside from mutual affection and attunement, involves the hope that the comforting will be internalized and help the child grow into a person secure enough to be self-protective.

Of course, some situations call for intervention—for instance, when a child cries for hours or remains listless in a corner for a long time. But in general, children don't need to be pushed or rushed into transitions or adaptations unless an actual disaster is in progress. The parent who, instead, needs a shy child to be assertive *now* might well shame the child by putting down the shyness as silly. Shame does harm, and traumatic harm done to a child's self-image and self-worth can cause complications later on—in some cases becoming entrenched in anger, depression, opposition, and addiction.

Raising children developmentally includes the notion that children and parents can grow together through experience and mutuality. In fact, parenting, according to this view, includes modeling more than preaching, and respect more than commands. Of course there are lessons to be taught and learned (such as physical safety and not hitting), but so much of what is taught is also through modeling respect and making room for each other's points of view. In the varied exchanges that occur in family settings, there can be room for negotiation and for the child's contributions to be respected, at the very least. Much of parenting can actually be creative and even enjoyably so. Children and parents teach each other, through play and imagination, to cope with so many feelings and experiences.

As an example of the crucial role of play within a family setting, a little boy I know would invite his parents to a "potty party" when he was age two and a few months and was addressing the prospect of cozying up to actual toileting. His parents went along with his fantasy play, bringing along a toy and a book while he sat and they talked. He would say, "Okay, I'm done," and they would all pack up (even though he hadn't left anything behind). One day he pee-peed right into the toilet, and so began another phase of life. But he had invented a way of "playing" through the anxiety that often surrounds toilet training. It also helped that the parents didn't insist on obedience or production (literally).

Let us not forget: the developmental approach applies to parents as well. Nobody is born a parent; parenting is learned. Each of us comes to parenthood with a specific past that can make us susceptible to blame, shame, anger, and more and therefore can influence our parenting style and the quality of our emotional growth in the parenting role. Parents, too, deserve a generous and humanizing attitude from the rest of us, who need to rein in our tendency to expect the impossible.

The popularization of parenting models in the media can place a lot of pressure on parents; we as a culture tend to want a parent to be sensitive but not hovering, to be involved but not a helicopter parent, to prevent his or her child from being bullied or becoming a bully. This kind of pressure can exploit parents' tendency to feel guilty and self-conscious, which can be rampant in a climate that highlights appearing strong and in control over acknowledgment of weakness and being overwhelmed. We need to recognize that many parents are doing the best they can and need help, not only to better attune to their kids but also so friends, neighbors, fellow citizens can better attune to them. Parenting, a bumpy road at best, was never meant to be a solitary expedition. We all lose it sometimes, and as parents, we need people to lean on who can support us in a variety of ways.

In moments of confusion and despair as parents, we may feel tempted to give up on trying to be sensitive to our children and ourselves; it can feel exhausting and even impractical. Besides reaching out for support, we may need some faith as well. I mean faith here not necessarily as religious belief but as faith in the developmental process itself—for instance, trust that the behavior we see in our child in this moment—the tantrum, the meltdown, the fears and anger—will pass. Indeed, when we see a child come together after collapsing emotionally and we see ourselves come back together as well, that trust is strengthened.

When I sometimes talk about psychotherapeutic work as spiritual in nature, I mean it in this sense of faith or trust: choosing an action without immediate evidence that the action will lead to constructive change. Using the developmental approach, in therapy as in parenting, requires a certain amount of suspended judgment. If I see a thread of meaning or purpose or even just sense its essence in what the client is presenting, I try to guide the therapeutic work along those lines. And yes, more evidence that we are progressing on a good path typically appears. (Besides, if we see we are mistaken, we can always change course, right?)

With some of my therapy clients, the evidence of progress has taken a long time to show up and my faith in the developmental approach has been tested. Some years ago, a young man named Emmett was brought in for therapy by his mother because of his lack of interest in school and his intensive use of marijuana. He was eighteen at the time and in his senior year of high school. For the first few months of sessions, Emmett mostly railed against his parents' selfish and punishing ways. He was determined not to change his own ways unless his parents changed theirs.

The understory was that Emmett so yearned for affection from his parents that it was tough for him to accept their unwillingness to work on their anxiety and unreliability. It was tough for me as well, since my way of doing therapy is typically family-oriented, even with adolescents when it seems necessary. In this case, the parents were not at all interested or inclined to engage in therapy for themselves or with Emmett.

Through all this time, Emmett had made no obvious progress. He didn't graduate from high school, and his showing up at appointments was haphazard. He continued to rage about and toward his parents in and out of therapy sessions. I had to give up on my own expectations of progress, let alone fast progress. I realized that his anxieties, in addition to his daily use of weed, were impeding both concentration and motivation. It was tempting to be firm, to say I would stop the sessions if he cancelled or didn't show up one more time. Nevertheless, I occasionally sensed the beginnings of traction and perhaps hope for him. And he continued to show up, if sporadically. So I waited.

Indeed, eventually he allowed himself to feel his grief about his parents' inability to be different from what they were. He began to show sparks of desire to reclaim pieces of his healthier parts, such as humor and perceptiveness, which had been dormant, buried by his depression and sense of alienation. He also began talking—feverishly at first—about troubling episodes in his past about which he felt guilty and for which he blamed only himself. In particular, at age ten, he had played doctor a few times with his girl cousin of the same age. This material was a far cry from his earlier insistence on blaming his parents. The real issue, it turned out, was not his parents' inconsistency so much as his self-hatred and fear of being seen as bad for what he had done. His shame prevented him from asserting himself in social situations with his peers, and then at home he would "relax, and do nothing," saying a kind of "fuck you" to his parents and their expectations of his being someone he wasn't.

Yet he started to glean from therapy some faith that he could in time find fun in work (and we were working, in our way) and in learning. He was moving toward more realistic expectations about his goals; life was no longer devastatingly grim, since he saw himself changing, even if gradually. The fact that he eventually started showing up emotionally for the sessions affirmed that being authoritarian with him wouldn't have been the way; it had already been attempted.

In essence, we were working developmentally, picking up where he had been stuck as a small child. We could work out some sense of his feeling validated for both his perceptions and his emotions, and he could be gently pushed toward exploring what was really going on inside him rather than settling into hate or blame.

A major aim of the developmental approach to childrearing is raising a child to develop an inner sense of safety— to be able to trust his or her own experience and feel at home within himself or herself. Specifically, this means having enough internal flexibility to deal with stresses and new circumstances and conflicts while continuing to mature throughout his or her life. The more safe we feel within, the less we are divided from ourselves, and so we are less inclined to project and create disconnects with others.

Central to developing inner safety is helping the child to know, label, and manage the flood of his or her feelings, so the child can learn that not every feeling needs to be acted upon. Here even fairy tales can play a crucial role. In his book *The Uses of Enchantment: The Meaning and Importance of Fairy Tales*, Bruno Bettelheim points out that, early on, children are overwhelmed by the experience of having mixed feelings toward one grownup. Especially before the age of five (though the specific age differs from child to child), children can find it hard to grasp that they can love and hate the same person.

The fairy tale helps because it simplifies emotions, presenting them in primary colors, as it were. The hero is all good, the villain is all bad. Evil is temporary and can be defeated. The child-turned-prince or -princess (in terms of identifying with the hero) can fight for autonomy, for a productive life outside the wretched confines of the forest—in a castle, perhaps.

Bettelheim writes: "When all the child's wishful thinking gets embodied in a good fairy; all his destructive wishes in an evil witch; all his fears in a voracious wolf; all the demands of his conscience in a wise man encountered on an adventure; all his jealous anger in some animal that pecks out the eyes of his archrivals—then the child can finally begin to sort out his contradictory tendencies."[3]

The child is helped to navigate ownership of harsh emotions—admitting to hate, for example—gradually and thus more safely. As the child's cognition expands, having opposing emotions toward a single person becomes palpable and bearable. The understanding is that the same child, after turning adult, will be better equipped at integrating emotional ambivalence. This in turn makes having more complex relationships with other people possible.

When you think about it, the inability to tolerate emotional ambivalence is a great problem in contemporary times. If we are not helped to navigate the developmental stage of reconciling the presence of good and bad in a single person—as well as its corollary, that there is both good and evil in all of us—we may be compelled to always have something or someone outside us that must be fought, condemned, gotten rid of. When we insist on hating one person or one country all the time and loving another all the time, we retreat to the age of the fairy tale and often remain there. And when we project our own evil parts onto bad leaders—or, let's say, axes of evil—there is no room to humanize them, to equalize the playing field, or to consider the parts of us that hold the very traits we see in them.

Living in a society that elevates celebrity and fame, we are easily seduced into attributing magic powers to a leader and expecting him or her (or them) to cure all our ills, or idolizing actors and sports heroes and living vicariously through them. The magic of the fairy tale, in these cases, becomes installed in the psyche (both individual and collective) and fails to evolve into realism about our own abilities and limits. When we see through the magical thinking and allow the rich and famous to step down from the pedestal where we installed them, we are on our way to recovering our own capacities for passion and enjoyment, for vivid engagement in love and life. We settle into ourselves. Claiming our own vitality is central to embracing the development of ourselves, our children, and our world. In a word, we become the heroes and heroines of our own lives.

5
The Cost of Belonging at Any Cost

Humans are designed to live in groups and to feel that we belong. It's part of how we are wired. When we belong to a group where we are accepted and respected, we feel comfort expressing our feelings, embracing our own position without shame. Even if we have cause to change our opinions in the back-and-forth with others, we can do this without losing our sense of stability. As we move in the world we carry with us the strength of the environment to which we have belonged—family, group, religion, country—and which has been our home. As such, we can face the world with a kind of security we can never have if we are always estranged from those around us.

In the climate of modern Western culture, where qualities such as independence, solitary bravery, and self-determination are key values, it becomes easy to overlook the importance of belonging. Indeed, not only in the United States, but in many places all over the globe, the ongoing trend has been to become an individual who can change affiliations, who can leave one's home behind to start anew. We are used to going where the job is or the university is and sometimes going where the dream beckons.

Being enamored of freedom and what it can yield, we may minimize our need to belong because it appears to constrain us, and sometimes the constraint is all we see. Indeed, belonging, whether in a couple or a family or a company or institution, requires a certain compromising of self. Things won't be exactly the way they would be if you were on your own, since at least some of the time the values or needs of other people take priority or at least must be taken into account.

However, this view ignores the fact that the need to belong is hardwired into humans. Being shunned is a core fear that, since ancient times, has driven us as individuals to adapt to our society, our tribe. Words such as "estranged," "alienated," "outcast," and "outsider" tend to evoke pain, and with it, a yearning for their opposite.

When we reckon ourselves to be independent and bury the yearnings to belong, they can sometimes take us over without our even knowing. On the one hand, our sense of belonging can be portable when we belong in our own skin. On the other hand, we may not recognize the undertow of yearnings for belonging in external ways if we have buried them. Just as we become more susceptible to the power of emotions we attempt to deny, so the urge to belong, when denied, can cause us to crave, consciously or unconsciously, a rescue operation brought to us by someone who promises to really understand us.

For most of us, our family of origin provides our first human climate. As such, family is where we first learn about terms of belonging, and the family's version of security and safety. If basic trust was broken or traumatized during childhood and the need to belong was not optimally met in that family context, we may deny this basic need, pushing it into our shadows. Then, if someone offers us absolute and unconditional belonging, we can be tempted to accept, even if it means going against our values. We may feel compelled to join groups or follow trends to the point of losing our freedom to think and feel, let alone act genuinely. This is one of the costs of belonging at any cost.

Yielding to the pressure to belong can look like conforming to the mentality of the time, even if it is a fad that will fly away almost as soon as it lands. If having a child who shows independence is a measure of belonging, a parent may feel the need to prove that his or her child is independent from an early age. So a mother may drop off her young child at the door of the nursery school with no more than a one-liner: "Mommy's going shopping"—ignoring the child's, and her own, real feelings and missing the opportunity to make the hardship of separating a shared experience. Alternatively, acknowledging the child's emotions and her own doesn't cripple either mother or child; on the contrary, it solidifies a bond that is reliable and honest. In addition, it does not leave the child in isolation, as if he or she were the only one missing out. It lays the groundwork for mutuality in future experiences of separation as well.

Susanna, a woman with whom I worked, was unknowingly rushing to find her own sense of belonging through trying to make her children and herself measure up to the social standards of a community they had recently moved into. Susanna pushed and pushed for her daughter, Rosie, to choose the academic track in high school, which presumed attending a four-year college as the goal. This was despite Rosie's giving clear signs of resistance through low grades, complaints of boredom in academic classes, and strong interests in learning a trade. But they were in a suburb of New York City, a posh one in Westchester County, where Susanna sought, at times frantically, a sense of fitting in. She joined a country club even though it was too expensive for her pocketbook, and signed her kids up for any activity that offered the possibility of making friends, aiming at keeping up one way or another. It was only when Rosie flunked out of college and was too depressed to continue that Susanna relented and started to examine, in therapy sessions, her own feelings of failure to belong.

Michael Chabon, in his Pulitzer Prize–winning novel *The Amazing Adventures of Kavalier and Clay*, explores what I see as the backstory to Susanna's issues concerning belonging. The novel deals mainly with the golden age of comics and the writers of comics in the 1940s in New York City and also the post–World War II yearning among its characters to find a new life. Chabon describes how the entry of suburbia on the scene at that time, fifty years before Susanna's story, coincided with a longing to escape the chaos that people felt was New York City, a longing that operated also in many families that were filled with immigrants' economic, social, and personal conflicts and separations. Chabon writes, "They sighed, and felt that one of the deepest longings in their hearts might one day soon be answered. Their families were chaotic things, loud and distempered, fueled by anger and the exigencies of the wise-guy attitude, and since the same was true of New York City itself, it was not hard to believe that a patch of green grass and a rational floor plan might go a long way to soothing the jangling bundles of raw nerves they felt their families had become."[4]

People were in a mad rush to "make it," to please the boss or do whatever it took to be able to open their checkbook and purchase a house that provided the safety of picnics without intruders. This, sadly, became the perfect setting where genuine desires, conflicts, opinions, and passions could die or be buried in favor of proving one's worth. Conformity, a form of belonging, was "in"—big time. People started buying and buying houses with pools and looking at each other across gated fences, determined to show only the neatest of exteriors of both home and self, and little of the mess inside.

Many women felt not only pushed into the fashionable conventions of motherhood but also pressured to prove the maturity of their children, to train them in everything for everyone to see, at the cost of intimacy. Chabon describes a mother walking down the hall to look at her sleeping son and then an unexpected tenderness coming over her as she gazes at him: "For several years she had been wishing him, willing him, into maturity, independence, a general proficiency beyond his years, as if hoping to skip him like a stone across the treacherous pond of childhood, and now she was touched by a faint trace of the baby in him."[5]

Like Susanna, the mother in this story was consumed by the need to prove her belonging to her social circle by adhering to its cultural standards. This was at the cost of acknowledging, even to herself, her genuine empathy for her son. As such, her son was learning to accommodate to his mother's expectations at the cost of his own genuine desires and needs.

The need to conform to the culture's expectations can run so strongly in us that it's nearly impossible for an individual to resist it on his or her own. We are up against a lot.

⁓ ᵃ

One of the most expensive costs of belonging at any cost involves the hazards of addiction, buttressed by the reliability of the patterns that come with it. For even though addiction can be terribly dangerous, it can also provide a set of adaptations that become familiar and may thus seem safe, even as they mask the chaos and hopelessness within. The world surrounding the addiction has its own climate, patterns, standards, and rules. And it can sometimes feel easier to choose the certainty of that world, or its appearance of certainty, over the uncertainties and absence of easy categories in a life without addiction.

A friend, Aaron, was an alcoholic, actively so for twenty years. He went through a divorce when his wife found out, and then he went for treatment and to Alcoholics Anonymous. Then he reunited with his wife, and then he blamed her for all of it. Their two sons wanted no part of what they saw as a psychodrama, and even though they were attached to their father, they kept their distance, hoping the situation would resolve. But the pattern continued: separating, AA and therapy, reuniting, and blaming. As awful as it was, it was also reliable. It was predictable and thus normal for Aaron and also for his family: "There he goes again." Like a soap opera, there were enough highs and lows to keep one's interest, but nothing really happened, so there had to be just enough emergencies to keep it interesting.

The predictability of being addicted to a substance or a person can mask loneliness and emptiness. Facing the loneliness and emptiness can feel more impossible than dealing with the hazards of the addiction, which is one reason why addictions aren't easy to give up.

I worked with a young girl named Autumn whose constant habit of starting fights with her younger sister,

Teresa, did seem like a kind of addiction. She couldn't tolerate any down time. She was bright and curious at school, but at home she was tense and almost always ready for a fight. At some point early in her treatment, I asked her pointedly why she always seemed to feel the need to start in with her sister. She answered: "But Carol, you don't get it. Maybe you don't know what it's like to always worry about being hit, like all of a sudden. It's so much easier when I start it. Then I don't have to sit and worry about what is going to happen. Did you ever think of that?"

I had thought of that, I had read about it, but Autumn said the words without apology, which got me to really understand without confusion. This is an example of how inducing trauma and abuse can become addictive to the abuser. When we are the ones who start the trouble, we can control the anxiety and we can cause the pain, instead of waiting in suspense, feverishly unsafe and in a panic, for it to arrive.

Autumn and I worked on predictability and her having a say in the therapy room to help her create tools to use when she felt that anxiety coming on. Fortunately, her family was open enough to engage in this process with her, which allowed her to move constructively out of the ritualized pattern.

~

We live in a culture where manipulation of our moods and choices is chronic. The news, industry, sales, and political interests bombard us with stimuli to influence us to buy into whatever they are selling. To construct their marketing messages, they're using information about how the human psyche works, including our need to conform in order to feel we belong. They can manipulate our longings and hungers, and before we know it, we can find ourselves making choices we might otherwise consider irrational.

What's more, if we are manipulated to the point where we feel we're part of a group that is beyond reproach, we may be on our way to buying into joining a cult. The word "cult" may sound too strong, but as it turns out, it isn't that hard for the word to apply more broadly than obviously destructive, even genocidal cults such as ISIS. We assume that those who join a group like ISIS lose their conscience, while the rest of us are immune to the seduction of cult thinking. In fact, the more arrogant we are about not being susceptible to cult thinking and the more we dismiss our need to belong, the easier it is for us to be seduced because we're not cautious enough about who is influencing us and why. One of our tasks, then— really, it's an obligation—is to investigate the sources of the pressures on us to think and behave in a certain way, so we can interrupt our tendencies to blindly follow the leader or the hype of the moment.

In *Quiet Horizon: Releasing Ideology and Embracing Self-Knowledge*, narrative psychotherapist Greg Jemsek takes the reader on the journey he went through in a Hindu cult in the 1970s. Jemsek calls attention to the terrible insult a child can sustain at the hands of a culture that injures feelings of well-being. He understands and has studied the effects of ridicule of children for their mistakes or their differences. When any of us is wounded in such a way, we can spend a lifetime trying to fill the deep holes of emotional emptiness. Jemsek knows all too well how an ideology can substitute, if inadequately and ultimately dangerously, for the absence of belonging and inner safety that therapists recognize as narcissistic damage. He writes: "Waiting in the wings for a person with narcissistic damage are individuals and organizations only too ready to provide him with that identity. False identities provided by predatory organizations are available in every direction, ready to secure the allegiance, money, and obedience of anyone still trying to sort out who he really is."[6]

I have a good friend, Annette Stephens, who was in a cult called Kenja, in Australia, for ten years. Her book, *The Good Little Girl*, describes each phase of her involvement in the cult, including what happened before and after.[7] A central element for her was having felt estranged in her life—from her husband, from a sense of purpose, and from real community. She shows us through her own painful journey how the belief that you have been found, recognized, and understood by someone having authority and what seems like unending power can be—well, addictive, definitely.

Annette had felt lost, overwhelmed, and alone, especially in terms of her parenting skills. She had attended a meeting about how to become a better parent, and that was the hook. The organization told her, if you come with us and leave your children for a time, you will become a better mother. The head of Kenja offered her safety and temporary freedom from the turmoil and loneliness she was experiencing in motherhood. He offered her understanding, acceptance, and belonging, promising to "cure" her and send her back to her family as a great mother. He preyed on her vulnerability.

My first reaction to reading Annette's story was sorrow and wanting to stop her from sinking, "knowing" it could never happen to me. As the pages moved and I moved through them, however, my feelings changed. They changed to the extent that I cried not from sadness about her but from feeling connected to her struggle and realizing I could have been in her shoes. I felt humble, realizing something like this could happen to any one of us.

But wait—please. It did happen to me. I didn't have to look far into my own history to find kinship to Annette's story. It happened as soon as I began psychotherapy when I was twenty-two. It was not that long after I had met and fallen in love with Lino, who would become my husband, and I was feeling shaky about committing to a long-distance relationship—he in Italy and I in the United States. So a friend set me up with a therapy appointment with someone with a pedigree suggesting he was a well-trained analyst. I was frightened and vulnerable, so I took to heart the words he uttered with authority. After all, it seemed like he was going to save me.

During my second private session with this therapist, he told me that I hated my mother. Period. Simple. He seemed to know this without hesitation. I sat there frozen.

Since he said it with such authority, then it must be so, even if it didn't resonate. In response, I was supposed to free-associate, to say whatever came to my mind—except that my response took a very long time for me to unwind, and even then I was reluctant to disagree with his absolute certainty about my hating my mother. I turned off access to the recesses of my vulnerability and rage, which would have been my genuine response, because that would have gone counter to his program.

I continued to see this therapist for a decade, as at the time I didn't grasp that I deserved to feel safer than I did on the inside, nor did I question the authority he clearly assumed. I was also in his therapy group, where his stance of superiority induced in the attendees a kind of groupthink. He threatened anyone who wanted to leave—in my case saying: "You're afraid to deal with what's going on with your relationships, and it's coming to a head, and you want to leave now?" The rest of the group colluded, which became its own kind of belonging. As it happened, I managed to escape the group and the private sessions years before I realized how cult-like the situation was. I had an excuse—by that time I had become a new parent. You may be thinking: How weak could she be? I'd never fall for that. I say: Let us be careful what we swear to.

～ొ

For people who have been stuck, whether in addiction, codependency, or a cult, in order to belong, breaking out is no small task. Giving up a predictable set of solutions can throw a person into chaos, which can lead to panic and shame—all the more so if the person's immediate human climate is not conducive to admission of mistakes. In some cases, people are scared for their physical safety if they should leave and so find themselves physically and emotionally trapped.

Breaking free may mean sitting with one's loneliness until one feels more connected within, and that can be a start. It is tempting to say that it takes a village, because in truth nobody grieves alone. And grieving is involved whenever we leave behind any kind of belonging, even when we leave aspects of an identity or an attachment behind that were, in actuality, choking us, or a lie. I also think that nobody really grows alone. And grieving is also an act of growing.

To begin creating a human climate in which we can afford to face the more difficult and inconvenient truths, we need to evolve in terms of facing our mistakes and having the supports to do so. To talk out loud about the fears and contradictions we feel and face, we need a sense of belonging somewhere in our universe. The most basic sense of belonging may well be a feeling of being at home inside ourselves, no matter what we have done, have thought of doing, or have had the impulses to do.

6

The Bully and the Brain Freeze

Have you ever known someone who was treated badly by someone close—a parent, a spouse, a boss—yet when telling you about it took the side of the person mistreating them? I've known several such people, both clients and friends. It always came as a surprise to witness a person who was otherwise intelligent, perceptive, and capable suddenly "lose" those skills when they talked about a key personal relationship. They seemed to be taken in by the other person's manipulations, and the power gap present in all bullying was in evidence.

I'm thinking of one friend whose husband would shout at her, sometimes even in public. When she would ask him to lower his voice, he would object, saying she was too sensitive. After observing this a few times when Lino and I were with them at a party or restaurant, I brought it up with her one day over coffee. She confided that he did this a lot, even when he was on the phone with her, and loudly enough that people around her could hear him through her phone.

Then she added, to my amazement, "He must be right, I'm too sensitive." Whatever *he* said seemed to have top billing, as if he had a monopoly on the truth.

My first response was the sensation of impatience rising up in me, along with the thought: "How can she be so clueless?" But of course we tend to be smarter about someone else's behavior than our own.

This relationship dynamic has a unique fingerprint that I call "the bully and the brain freeze." One partner is controlling and intimidating, and the other is passive to the point of emotional absence. The giveaway is usually a glassy look, suggesting surrender, that accompanies the person's defense of the bully's behavior. Rather than owning his or her right to be upset and stating it out loud—to someone else if not directly to the bully—it is as if the person on the receiving end has become paralyzed, like a deer in the headlights, and his or her brain has become frozen.

Given my tendency to approach things developmentally, when I see this behavior, I start to wonder if the current bullying situation might be triggering a memory of a past instance of bullying or shaming. The extreme passivity in such instances can have something to do with how the person interpreted, or was pushed to interpret, the earlier incident as his or her own fault. Internalized blame can cause a kind of paralysis—a brain freeze—that makes processing the present event overwhelming. We remain stuck in the dependent position, unable to stand up for our own integrity, which in that moment can seem quite foreign.

I say "we" because this kind of internal division between ourselves and our power can happen to any of us, and I am no exception. As a child, when one of my older brothers, whom I had put rather on a pedestal, exploded in sudden disapproval, I would "lose my English," as I called it, and become quite inarticulate, as if words were not something I had at my disposal. This response came to haunt me in later situations, when, according to my internal warehouse of emotional memories, others talking to me with intensity or authority evoked a response of apprehension and fear. I had to do a lot of work on this issue (in and out of a therapist's office). The same dynamic haunts many of us as we feel threatened by experts, peers, politicians, lovers, children; we lose perspective and the capacity to assert our right to make up our own mind.

To clarify: The bully and the brain-freeze pattern involves bullying, but of a particular type. In bullying you can see the victim trying to avoid the experience, for instance, by running away, as from physical threats or racial slurs, or by trying to befriend the bully. In the bully and the brain freeze, the victim has almost no awareness that bullying is going on. The victim assumes the bully is right, so it must not be bullying. But this is wrong; abuse is abuse and bullying is bullying, even if the bully is right about the facts.

The dynamic of the bully and the brain freeze is almost always complex and layered. In fact, frequently the brain-frozen person also has a certain power over the bully, and the bully is also stuck in the recurring pattern. As an example, I'll tell you about Lucas, who came to see me because he felt trapped in his marriage. His wife, Jane, was in many ways a nag, constantly telling Lucas he wasn't cutting it as a father and berating him for being "unwilling to grow up"—a phrase she repeated often. When he was considering divorce and voiced this to her, she shot back at him with righteous certainty: "Married once, married forever." She blamed him for not giving the marriage enough of a try.

Lucas was competent in business and often spoke before large audiences without a glitch. Yet in the face of Jane's berating, he found himself unable to counter her arguments. When they spoke together in my office, his words left him, and any sense in the room of his right to be in doubt about the marriage disappeared as well.

As Lucas and I explored his background in private sessions it was not that hard to find old patterns that were being triggered in the present. His parents had divorced when he was eight, and his relationship with his mother, who had raised him, had been suffocating. He was supposed to be the man of the house and to therefore follow rules that his mother continuously threw his way—though without explanation and often punctuated with comments about his not being a "good-enough boy." As much as he had felt frozen back then and artificially respectful of his mother's demands, he was now frozen in the presence of his wife's anger.

However, the power differential was not so clear-cut. Yes, Jane was the bully, and Lucas felt abused by her and powerless. Yet Lucas provoked his wife as well. His tendency to withdraw emotionally made her feel isolated. His passivity and tongue-tied-ness left her feeling powerless, which enraged her, making her more prone to attack him. Although Lucas disliked Jane's nagging, his withdrawing gave him a sense of power in the relationship. He would retreat to catch his breath and then wait a couple of days before even greeting her in passing. It was his way of one-upping her. This was not exactly conscious, but Lucas well knew that Linda's Achilles' heel was her own fear of abandonment. This dynamic left them stuck in a tangle of mutual resentment and emotional distancing.

To the extent that his own early anger had never been metabolized or expressed, it remained in his shadows—in his basement. For this to change, Lucas had to override the old messaging that feeling anger made him a bad person and see that he was worthy of experiencing anger, both inside and out loud. This became the focus of our therapy work. As he learned to be more forthcoming with his emotions, Jane was less on guard and could be more relaxed and not have to stay in the bullying position. Lucas could then experience being listened to and gain more comfort in the relationship as well.

Whenever one person changes his or her part of the relational dynamic, there is always a shift or reaction on the other's part. For that shift to be conducive to growth, however, takes the work of both parties. In this particular case, both Lucas and Jane were open to changing and being affected by each other in constructive ways, and so the relationship improved.

When someone takes on the role of bully, it's often the case that underneath that behavior lies a shaky sense of self-esteem. Inducing helplessness and humiliation in another person can give the bully a temporary sense of superiority and power. If the bully not only has fragile self-esteem but is also disconnected from authentic emotions and intentions, it's as if he or she is running on empty in terms of purpose or energy. This person may then turn to another to fill that emptiness, at which point he or she becomes what I call a vampire—not a vampire in the classic sense, of course, but an emotional vampire.

An emotional vampire is someone who feels fundamentally lonely and grabs onto whoever is easily available, invading the emotional space of that person in order to come alive emotionally himself or herself. The vampire obviously has emotions of his or her own, but they go unrecognized. They have been too difficult or too unbearable to process, so they are pushed down into the shadows.

To illustrate this, let me share what happened regarding a client of mine, Carla, and her elderly mother, Veronica. Carla came to see me because no matter how hard she tried, she couldn't deal with her mother without feeling guilty, angry, or depleted.

Carla described experiencing a state of brain freeze (she didn't call it that) some of the time. For one thing, sometimes her mother seemed so innocent and in need of support that it was hard for Carla to see why she felt so drained and generally resentful after being with her. For another, Carla frequently could not find the words to respond adequately to her mother's criticisms. Carla's brain freeze with her mother was in distinct contrast with her work as a teacher and her roles as a mother and wife, arenas in which she felt quite competent and clear-headed.

Carla was an only child, lived in the same town as her mother, and visited her three evenings a week plus Sundays. However, the things Carla did to be helpful were often belittled by her mother as no big thing. Worse, Veronica would often point out to Carla how other daughters were really close with their mothers—they helped their mothers out of love, not obligation. For Carla, it felt like she was damned if she did, damned if she didn't.

It might sound odd to describe an elderly woman like Veronica, presumably weak and innocent, as a vampire. Yet what appeared to fill her up emotionally was not the attention and care her daughter was offering but the criticism she herself was dishing out.

If Veronica was a vampire sucking Carla's energy, initiative, and feelings of self-worth, then slaying that vampire would seem to be in order. Ouch, indeed. Not actually slaying her mother, of course, but killing the power her mother held over her. Even so, Carla's initial response to my idea of "slaying the vampire" was less than enthusiastic: she didn't want to be the bad guy. She also sensed her mother's inherent fragility—that her mother could collapse or disintegrate if their dynamic changed. At the same time, Carla's emotional weariness was intensifying. She understood that her mother was the victim of her own congested emotions as well as fear of grief and of life, and she wanted to help her—yet she also had to protect herself. Through our sessions, she saw that she couldn't really feel generosity or love toward her mother unless she drew some boundaries against her mother's invasion of her emotional space.

The turning point was when Carla mentioned to her mother that she was seeing a therapist, to which Veronica barked, "That's ridiculous. You'll see, it will do you more harm than good." This angered Carla, who was seeing more and more just how invested her mother was in remaining bitter. As Carla started realizing she could still be a decent person if she got angry (even very angry), she started to feel more comfortable about setting limits. She learned to put a halt to her mother's barrage about how inadequate she was as a daughter by saying, "Look, I'm doing the best I can, and I'm not going to compete with anyone else." When she told her mother firmly but without spite that if she criticized her she would leave early that day, Veronica began to see that her daughter was serious and determined—at which point the dynamic between them began to shift.

Surprisingly for Carla, and even for me, Veronica's self-absorption began to soften some. One day when Veronica told Carla she was feeling down as usual, Carla responded with a funny, somewhat pointed one-liner, "Why should tonight be different?" to which Veronica actually cracked a smile. Whereas their interactions in the past had been recyclings of the same lines and dramatic stances, now there was a bit of air, as in emotional circulation and the possibility for a more genuine exchange. Truth be told, there began to be more aliveness in the relationship, with a little bit of fighting that was similar to play.

Even so, no one can expect a vampire-type to go lightly into the sunset. People who bully others usually find that role reliable, even addictive, so a certain amount of leverage is required to persuade them to even think about relinquishing it. The first sign of leverage is when the victim is ready to set limits or disengage from the relationship altogether, yet that is often not enough. In fact, when anyone—in any situation, not just with a vampire—is setting a limit where none was set before, he or she needs to be prepared with multiple strategies. If you are intending to stand up for your rights, have a backup plan for when the first attempt doesn't work. All too often, people walk away defeated when the child or husband or whoever seems unfazed or oppositional, thinking, "Well, that didn't work."

Setting a limit with a certified bully or vampire also requires cultivating endurance so as to not crumble on the spot. Carla and I needed to work on her perseverance. She was fearful of connecting with her own assertiveness and her anger at being bullied. The guilt feelings about being aggressive with an elderly woman bothered her for a while, but eventually she discovered that she actually felt like a nicer person when she wasn't being smothered. She also got used to the idea that she, Carla, could be mean. Actually, she owned up to liking it some, particularly because it was a part of who she was, though not the whole picture.

～ぁ

The person experiencing a brain freeze may not only have trouble thinking clearly; he or she may also be immune to noticing a blatant and distressing fact—such as infidelity in a partner who is also the bully. This can happen even when friends and family see what is going on and point it out. Sometimes people unconsciously refuse to recognize what is right in front of them because, like most of us, they have been conditioned to believe that as soon as they know something, they have to act on it. But the prospect of taking action is frightening or overwhelming enough that they become frozen instead.

In cases of bullying involving danger or threat, taking immediate action may be crucial. But where there is no pending emergency, it is entirely legitimate to take the time to pause and see more clearly what is going on without being obligated to act. I made up the term "the space between clarity and action" to describe this freedom to move more slowly. We are entitled to find and claim the space that does in fact exist between gaining clarity about a situation and taking action about it—as in, say, leaving a relationship. You don't always have to act right away on what you have come to know. You can be confused or ambivalent about what to do, and you can have the space to sit with the confusion or ambivalence, to process the decision—with support if you need it. In other words, you have permission to take your time.

As we have seen, there is a certain reliability to addictive behavior, and this is so even for the brain-frozen person. What looks like a terrible situation to outside observers may supply the comfort of sameness and predictability to the person experiencing it. Often a person who remains, frozen or otherwise, in a bullying relationship is also guarding against emotions, such as acute loneliness or despair, lying below the surface of the person's awareness that are even more painful than the person's feelings in response to the abuse that is going on. In addition, the pressure of guilt and anxiety about what will happen if he or she tries to alter the relationship dynamic can provoke its own kind of brain freeze. Even the suggestion that the situation should be tackled immediately can prompt a look of panic and a refusal.

Well-meaning family members or friends who keep encouraging the brain-frozen person to take action, such as leaving a relationship, can become tired of listening to the same story and resentful of trying to help when the obviously needed change still hasn't happened. If they have little interest in or patience for learning about the conflicted feelings at play and how these may be hampering the person's progress, the family member or friend or even therapist who is supposedly there to help and support can actually become a bully. The brain-frozen person may then pull away, avoiding contact for fear of being pestered about the situation and reminded of how messed up or stubborn he or she is to not make a change.

My own strong sense is that if we are to confront the kind of emotional impasses described here, we need supports. We need the company of people who can offer real interest in us, who are willing to get to hear about the complex dynamics that are at work. Sometimes this company may be a therapist, but not always. Certainly the more comfortable we become with talking out loud about the kind of support we need—that we need to be listened to, not to be lectured or prodded—the more other people can understand that they too, even if frozen, need supports that regard every human experience with dignity.

7
Visiting the Shadows: A Nod to Carl Jung

Central to the developmental approach to growing up is coming to know, integrate, and regulate our emotions so they don't dominate us. We have seen how emotions trump thoughts when they are congested or in some way hidden or out of control. We can also fear an emotion, whether because it wasn't safe to feel it as a child or because we associate it with shame, to name two reasons. When we fear or hate an emotion so much that we want to deny its existence, we unconsciously send it into what Carl Jung called the "shadow," a part of the mind outside our awareness.

When I came upon Jung's small volume *The Undiscovered Self* some ten years ago, its chapter "Self Knowledge" rather had me at hello, since it explained so clearly what

I had long felt to be true. Jung explains that underneath the persona that is who we believe we are lies a plethora of emotions we don't always know about. Often, these are emotions we were not helped to face and integrate as children, so they became taboo. Our self-concept—for instance, that we are good, moral, always bold, and so on—won't allow us to acknowledge emotions that don't fit under those labels, so we unknowingly bury those emotions in our shadows. (I like to use the plural "shadows" to convey the variety of forms and expressions of these feelings that have been relegated to the dark.)

People often assume that only our aggressive urges are concealed in the shadows. However, positive emotions can be hidden there, too. For example, people raised in a family climate where vulnerability and tenderness were shamed may unconsciously push their gentle side into the shadows.

Once relegated to the shadows, these emotions, being unexpressed, can fester. They may drive sudden emotional explosions that are triggered by situations reminiscent of the situation that caused them in the first place. More often, the denied emotions are unconsciously projected onto others. Sometimes they are projected onto people we regard as "other," who appear far from us culturally, physically, or even temperamentally, if not geographically. But just as often the projection occurs close to home—quite close, in fact.

Many people just about marry their shadows—that is, they marry someone who ends up driving them crazy (as they drive their spouse crazy) with faults that in fact reside in them. For example, if one partner carries anger in her shadows, she can be hyper-ready to notice anger in her partner, or even provoke it, and then accuse her partner of being angry. Meanwhile, her partner might carry, say, a tendency to depressed moods in his or her shadows that is projected onto her, such that the partner feels justified in accusing her of being a wet blanket, always spoiling the fun.

To engage in what Jung calls the "mutual withdrawal of projections" requires the willingness to take responsibility for those parts of ourselves we project onto other people. It also requires the willingness to examine our assumptions about being right when we blame others for our woes. Jung notes how this process involves a cycle of growth: Owning our shadows leads to realization of our imperfections, and as we become less judgmental about them, we can manage increasing degrees of truth about our fallibilities. Once we don't need to project our imperfections onto others as our first defense, we are freer to empathize with them. As empathy increases, we are not as insistent on combativeness, whether on a personal or a societal level.

In a particularly beautiful passage, Jung explains the connection between accepting our imperfections and being able to love. He says that human relationships are actually "based . . . on imperfection, on what is weak, helpless and in need of support—the very ground and motive of dependence. The perfect has no need of the other, but weakness has, for it seeks support and does not confront its partner with anything that might force him into an inferior position and even humiliate him."[8] Put another way, as we accept more fully our own flaws, we are less likely to want to humiliate someone else for theirs.

Not only individuals but also societies and even nations have shadows. Just as an individual does, a group or nation has a certain collective self-concept and buries collective emotions and memories it cannot afford to admit in its collective shadows. Jung's conviction is that societies seek scapegoats when they are unable or unwilling to look at their own shadows, and this is what has kept humanity engaged in hatred, divisions, and wars through history. And as a society or nation, we try to get rid of evil by projecting it onto other cultures or nations, or by declaring certain people to be evil and then seeking to export them literally, as in the deportation of immigrants (who are at times blamed for economic hardship and even terrorism). However, it is not possible to effectively rid ourselves of evil by "exporting" it, since some of it resides in us always. Projection may work in our imaginations temporarily, but it's a catch-22. As long as we hate the notion that we are capable of evil, we will, as Jung says, "prefer to localize the evil with individual criminals or groups of criminals, while washing our hands in innocence."[9]

Jung pushes us to see that we all have the capacity for both good and evil, that we are "all potential criminals."[10]

That is, under certain circumstances, any one of us can feel that combination of intense emotion, motivation, and adrenaline that could swerve into an act of sadism or enjoyment of observing such an act. In addition, he makes the case that we are obligated to deal with the legacy of evil handed to us by history. Our hope for bettering the present, and the future as well, can become more realistic only when we begin to own up to our own dual nature—our capacity for both good and bad.

Writing a few years after World War II, Jung saw the survival of the human race, threatened by the availability of nuclear weapons (and we can now add: the human acceleration of climate change), as the most urgent reason for us to deal with our collective shadows. He writes—wisely, I think—"It is not that present-day man is capable of greater evil than the man of antiquity or the primitive. He merely has incomparably more effective means with which to realize his proclivity to evil."[11] As somber and sobering as this statement may be, Jung also points to a solution when he stipulates that the work of integrating our shadows belongs front and center in its importance.

Although Jung discusses the crucial yet little-noticed role the shadows play at the collective level, he regards integrating our shadows as mainly an individual process. Indeed, shadow integration has been a central part of my own psychotherapy practice. One example is that of Jason, who was thirty-six and single when he came to see me for therapy. He came because of what he described as lack of motivation in relationships and in his job as a computer systems analyst. He missed his father, who had died in a drunk driving accident when Jason was ten. He blamed his mother for his father's death, which he felt was a suicide, if unconsciously so. He said his mother was "a bitch, a cold-hearted woman who should never have married or had kids, who enabled my father and made him want to drink." He remembered her nonstop warnings to his dad that she would leave if he continued drinking. "Why the hell didn't she, anyway? She had no backbone. It's no wonder that he wanted to off himself."

Although Jason's anger stayed focused on his mother, I wondered whether he might also be longing for the father he never had, or never had enough of. Even during his years of heavy drinking, Jason's father had functioned reasonably well as a high school English teacher, and over the years he had received letters from students and school officials testifying to how his students found him inspiring and encouraging. If Jason's father had been caught up more in his students' adoration than in his son, Jason might have felt resentment and jealousy that he then tried to disown. I kept this thought to myself early on, however, since pressing Jason to tackle all these shadow emotions at once would have paralyzed him or chased him away; it would also have been a violation of his own process.

So we moved gradually (that is, developmentally), beginning where Jason was: his disappointment with his own lack of accomplishment. As we got into Jason's anger at himself for not pursuing a graduate degree in something that really fascinated him, such as law, we began to explore his critical style with himself and others. One day, after a year of weekly therapy, he talked about his current girlfriend and how "it makes me crazy that she says she likes to drink, even though it's only socially and only sometimes." He added that he realized he was coming on too aggressively, that he was picking arguments with her, and that his anger was beginning to make him feel uncomfortable.

It wasn't hard to see the similarity between his and his mother's styles, and since we had established a pretty trusting relationship by then, I commented rather bluntly: "Wow, are you getting how much you sound like your descriptions of your mother?" At first he denied it could be possible—after all, he'd spent so many years hating her—to which I said, "Just because you spent all those years hating her doesn't mean you're not like her. In fact, that may be part of why you hate her."

Jason had a tough time at first with this glimpse of his shadows. Once he started to see the resemblance between his mother's behavior and his own, he began blaming himself as a due punishment. The truth was that he had no room in his repertoire for imperfections. A multiplicity of emotions toward both parents started to tumble out from his shadows, and we began to explore them.

It turned out that, as children often do, he blamed himself for his father's death, wondering if the stress of being his (Jason's) father had caused the fatal accident. Yes, his mother had nagged his father, but as a young kid, Jason had at times been irritable or cranky—as most children can be sometimes. Eventually, Jason came to see his anger toward his father—for drinking and, even more, for dying when Jason was so young. If his father had really cared about him, he would have taken better care of himself and stayed around, wouldn't he?

As Jason navigated his emotions about his parents, his hunger for forgiveness for his anger—both as a kid and toward his mother over the years—also surfaced. In beginning to forgive himself, Jason also began to long for some contact and real honesty with his mother. As happens so often, once the emotions squashed into the shadows became more freed up, more energy was available for Jason to put into his work and his relationships in general. He shared some aspects of his past with his girlfriend and explained how he was triggered in their relationship due to feelings related to his parents. He decided he needed some time on his own. He wasn't blaming her, he said, but he needed the space to come to better terms with the feelings he had hidden from himself for so long.

I first became keenly aware of my own shadows when I was fresh out of social work school and working in a residential treatment center. One of my less conscious motivations for becoming a psychotherapist was a wish to do unto others in ways I had not myself experienced as a child. Indeed, the vicarious healing of one's own emotional wounds through helping other people to heal theirs is not an uncommon motivation to become a therapist. However, things go south if the therapist basks in the superiority of being "the healer" and fails to examine his or her own issues and the projections they cause, even onto a client.

Projection onto a client is not alarming in itself. It's human nature, and it happens. But if it goes unexamined, it can become toxic—the therapist may even manipulate the therapy process unconsciously to suit his or her own unrecognized needs. If this should happen and either the client or the therapist points it out, it can be therapeutic for the therapist to own this phenomenon and apologize. None of this shadow work is easy, and it is sometimes even less so if we are in a helping role or profession and have sworn allegiance to do no harm.

In the beginning of my work as a therapist, I was aware only of my wish to do good. I soon realized that I also hoped to be, and to be seen as, a good person. This may have been because growing up, I had not particularly been known—at least in the confines of my family's apartment—as the sweet, good little girl but had exhibited my share of temperamental crankiness. So to be a social worker offered (in my imagination, anyway) an opportunity to feel like a good, helpful person and thus create a retelling of my earlier story.

One of my first jobs after earning my master's degree was at a residential treatment center for seriously emotionally disturbed youngsters. When I found myself working with Delia, an eleven-year-old resident who had been physically abused and neglected and now was suicidal, I felt terrible for her. I cried when I read her chart. On meeting and working with her, however, I discovered that she was skilled at enacting cruelty, perhaps to make other people feel as helpless as she had felt. It didn't seem that her motivation was conscious, and yet she glared at me with what seemed like a raging spite that embodied both enjoyment and hate. My compassion for her began to vanish. During our sessions, when I was the target of hurled insults and sometimes tissue boxes, I began to feel resentment and more—actually, way more.

From time to time, Delia became acutely suicidal; she said she wanted to jump out of a window and die. One dark afternoon I actually had the fantasy of leading her to the window of my fourth-floor office and offering to help her jump out. Yes, that's pretty despicable, I agree. I felt terrible about feeling this. But wait, there was more. It was all quite complicated.

After the session was over and I had some time to breathe, it came to me that my rage to the point of wanting to help Delia to her death was not only a consequence of her provocations; some aspect of me must have been triggered, and I needed to take a good look at this. Ouch, this seemed really big. There must have been quite a bit of anger in me for it to be so ready to be engaged.

As a young girl, Delia had been helpless in the hands of cruel and impulsive people, and she had learned cruelty through their modeling and through the urges of wanting to hurt them back. While it would no doubt take her a long time to admit her shadow side—in her case, her vulnerability and need and tenderness—if I were to help her, I had to feel less like a saint and more like an equal as another human being. My plans to be "the good one" had been foiled again.

Let me add that I was fortunate enough to be able to share these discoveries with my own therapist but in no way dared approach a supervisor with what in those days might well have been grounds for firing. Instead I was helped to realize that these were feelings, not actions, as well as a possible catalyst for change in Delia's therapy.

I improvised a treatment plan for Delia that included more honesty than I had originally intended or been taught (those were the days when the professional was supposed to keep a mighty and clinical distance). During our next session, I told Delia that she was capable of making me feel crazy and enraged and making me cry, and that I gave up—not on her but on winning any contest for control. What I offered her instead, which in fits and starts she began to accept, was a willingness to try to find out why she felt compelled to act this way and if life for her could be different.

I have often wondered if Delia accepted my offer not just because I had traveled to my own shadows but because I showed (unintentionally at first) that I was willing to feel and acknowledge the depth of my frustration with her. In addition, recognizing that the anger she provoked in me was my own made it possible for me not to use it against her or to retaliate.

At the opposite end of the psychotherapeutic spectrum, one might say, from Jungian work with the shadows is positive psychology. The term "positive psychology" was coined by Abraham Maslow—the humanistic psychologist famous for his hierarchy of needs, in particular, the need for self-actualization—in response to observing that psychologists paid too little attention to positive aspects of human behavior, such as growth and development. The idea and the label were made popular by psychologist Martin Seligman and eventually became a branch of psychology in its own right. Positive psychology is the study of what helps people live well and increase their positive experiences. Seligman feels (as did Maslow before him) that traditional psychology and psychotherapy have overstressed the negative experiences of childhood and that such a trend needs to be complemented by emphasis on strengths and growth.

Seligman goes further than Maslow, however, in terms of downplaying the relevance of what happens in childhood. In his book *Authentic Happiness*, Seligman writes: "I think that the events of childhood are overrated; in fact I think past history in general is overrated. It has turned out to be difficult to find even small effects of childhood events on adult personality, and there is no evidence at all of large—to say nothing of determining—effects."[12]

As I see it, a problem arises when positive experience is emphasized to the point of dismissing what has happened to a person developmentally. We may be advised: "Don't dwell on the past," but in fact the past dwells in us. We cannot amputate our past any more than we can amputate our shadows (which we cannot do). The effects of the past may be hidden, but they are never gone. The effects of past trauma, such as unacknowledged, unprocessed emotions, tend to fester when they are neglected. This may show up as a simple ambivalence toward life, though it can also evolve into disdain or rejection of whole categories of a person's experience or emotions. Or those who know they suffer leftover effects of trauma may keep those memories to themselves.

Barbara Ehrenreich, author and political activist, challenges not just positive psychology but the positive thinking approach in general. She began this project after encountering an unrelenting "positive" attitude from so many people, from health care professionals to peers and friends, when she had breast cancer. In an online blog for the *Guardian* titled "Smile! You've Got Cancer," she writes, "Like a perpetually flashing neon sign in the background, like an inescapable jingle, the injunction to be positive is so ubiquitous that it's impossible to identify a single source." Almost everyone she met seemed to insist that a positive attitude was essential to her recovery. The message was clear—too clear, as Ehrenreich states in the blog: that if cancer wins the battle "when positive thinking fails, . . . then the patient can only blame herself; she is not being positive enough; possibly it was her negative attitude that brought on the disease in the first place."[13]

Ehrenreich, who devotes an entire chapter of her book *Bright-Sided: How Positive Thinking Is Undermining America* to Martin Seligman, takes issue with his view of suffering. She sees it as judgmental and detached. She argues that in making positivity a key virtue, we are undermining the recognition of pain and trauma as real and valid experiences—which, in her view, also minimizes the need for social change. She links this outlook with the positive theology brand of Christianity, which advertises success as a prize for the worthy. Referring to some religious sermons, she says, "But always, in a hissed undertone, there is the darker message that if you don't have all you want, if you feel sick, discouraged, or defeated, you have only yourself to blame. Positive theology ratifies and completes a world without beauty, transcendence, or mercy."[14]

I tend to agree. The "positive" approach has a negative effect when it pressures us to hide our wounds, our traumas, our hates and loves in the shadows, from where they limit our experience without our being aware of it.

When we lose contact with our shadows, we not only sometimes marry them, we may go to war with them; sometimes we elect them to high office. In the case of the election of Donald Trump, for example, many on both sides of the political spectrum were fascinated by his Mafia-esque style, his bravado, his striking the pose of a superhero who has no need for reason or facts. This fascination occurs for many reasons, and one of them is that we all have that bully persona buried somewhere in our shadows. In liberals it tends to be less acknowledged because it doesn't fit with their self-image and tends to be more deeply buried than in conservatives.

For example, from time to time I have fantasized about having a Mafia member by my side (such as the fictional Tony Soprano) to help me get my way when I'm frustrated or even want to get back at someone (yes, it's true). The more I, as a liberal, get to know that character inside me, the less I experience myself as oh-so-superior to that raunchy, mean, entitled, and grandiose kind of person.

This is hard stuff because our first reaction to the idea that we are all potential bullies can be horrifying. No, we want to say, that can't be true. But consider how we sometimes root for the killer or the robber who is attractive or sexy or savage in movies. Owning our bullying potential becomes easier still if we see it not as a prison sentence but as just one among all our potential aspects, for good and otherwise.

Even though accepting that our shadows might have similarities with people we hate or disrespect is an uncomfortable struggle, moving in that direction is likely to be worth the effort. On the personal level, it can save marriages and parent-child relationships from drowning in negativity. On larger scales, it challenges us to question our tendency to hate, to revel in that hatred, or to gloat about how much better we are than the "other" group.

There is such a divide in the human climate, and so many of us, on both sides (liberals and conservatives), are engaged in projecting shadows onto each other. Not much is likely to be solved until we start to bridge that gap. And the more each of us processes our own shadows, the more we can be curious about other people and their points of view and how they got there.

Facing and then accepting and processing our darker, buried sides is by nature an uneven process, with failures alongside successes. Yet the more we engage in this process, the less likely we are to remain emotionally congested. This is because keeping what lies in the shadows from our awareness takes emotional energy that could be used in other ways. When the congestion is eased and that energy is freed up, we have more space inside us to process a variety of emotions, as well as to question our assumptions and interrupt our tendencies, all of which constitute a healthy condition we might call good emotional circulation.

It is when we bury feelings that they can control us or pop out in explosions that lead to blame, conflict, and at the collective level, even war. Carl Jung was in no joking mood when he said that the only way to avoid nuclear war was for us, person by person, row by row, and group by group, to take ownership of our own shadows. Even though there's no guarantee that it will work, at least the first time around, still, as Jung pointed out, it's the only way for us to make real progress.

8
Don't Know Much about History

I have always loved history, and unlike the line from the Sam Cooke song that serves as this chapter's title, I used to think I knew a fair amount about it. My earliest exposure to history was around age ten, when I got hooked on the Grosset & Dunlap Signature Books, a series of biographies of people such as Mozart and Pocahontas written for the younger reader. I would lie on my bed and daydream my way through those books, mesmerized by other people's loves and trials as I imagined being someone else living in a different time.

My grasp of history remained simplistic right through middle school and into high school. In history class my sophomore year, because I was good at memorization, review books came in handy as I prepared for tests, and man, did the authors of those books make history simple—a short list of reasons for the US entry into World War II, a streamlined description of how the sides in that war were drawn. But then I read Richard Hofstadter's *The American Political Tradition* in American history class during my junior year.

First published in 1948 by Alfred Knopf, the book held up well through the decades; both my kids read it in high school history class in the 1990s. I remember learning a lot from that book that made me sad. Most memorably, it punctured my idealized view of the Founding Fathers, especially when I learned that Thomas Jefferson had owned slaves, which to me was a tragic flaw. I don't remember any discussion in high school about the complexity of social issues in US history, or the fact that many upper-class white people at that time had slaves, or that white superiority was assumed all over America, even in parts of the country where slavery wasn't institutionalized.

What I'd learned in Hofstadter's book got hazy over time. However, I revisited the book recently, pulling it off a family bookshelf and opening its pages for old times' sake. When my eyes fell on the passage about Abraham Lincoln and his ambivalence about slavery, I felt sure I had never read it before, though I must have. Lo and behold, while there is no doubt about Lincoln's dislike of slavery and his eventual role in the emancipation of the slaves, on several occasions he came out quite clearly on the side of white superiority, a fact that probably surprises many of us (and perhaps mostly white people, at that).

During a speech in Charleston, South Carolina, in 1858, a few years before he became president and before the Civil War broke out, Lincoln said, "I will say, then, that I am not, nor ever have been, in favor of bringing about in any way the social and political equality of the white and black races (applause): that I am not, nor ever have been, in favor of making voters or jurors of negroes, nor of qualifying them to hold office, nor to intermarry with white people. . . . And inasmuch as they cannot so live, while they do remain together there must be the position of superior and inferior and I as much as any other man am in favor of having the superior position assigned to the white race."[15]

This speech was delivered in a Southern state, so perhaps Lincoln bent his remarks to suit the pro-slavery mentality of his listeners. It does seem that he said different things in different places and times, once saying in Peoria, Illinois, for instance: "No man is good enough to govern another man, without that man's consent."[16] Hofstadter explains that "Lincoln was *not* emphasizing the necessity for abolition of slavery in the near future; he was emphasizing the immediate 'danger' that slavery would become a nation-wide American institution if its geographical spread were not severely restricted at once."[17] Hofstadter also comments that Lincoln's efforts to come across as an abolitionist and then to appeal to those against it "involved him in embarrassing contradictions."[18]

Regardless of the reasons for his changeable stance, Lincoln, a key figure in this country's mythology, had just fallen from his pedestal in my world. I was forced to see that Lincoln was not the cardboard figure I had learned about as a child, with a single, fixed opinion about slavery, but a complex man whose views evolved over time and who, as a politician, could be calculating and opportunistic.

I had idealized him as much as I had idealized Jefferson, probably even more so (I know I'm not alone it this), and my sadness at discovering his conflicting views about race was reminiscent of the sadness I had felt years earlier when I learned about Jefferson owning slaves. This sadness cut deeply because it disturbed my identity as an American citizen and also as a white liberal and perhaps other identities I carry as well.

Our identity as members of any group, including our sense of belonging, is partly rooted in that group's history. It's almost ingrained in us as humans to align ourselves with the stories, key figures, beliefs, and values of the group or groups we belong to, especially the ones we are born into. This goes almost without saying. When we discover a disconnect between the group's values and our own, it challenges that alignment, that identification. This can be hard.

In my own case, to be honest with myself, I had to grieve this sadness, let go of some old assumptions, and expand what I thought I knew. In other words, I had to change.

As my eyes were opened wider about Lincoln, I was confronted also, and yet again, by the reality of racism in America. Although the antislavery North won the war over the proslavery South, it turns out there had been ambivalence about slavery in the North as well, with conflicting opinions about blacks gaining freedom and little thought given to the social and economic impact of emancipation. I had always thought of the abolition of slavery as a moral issue; now I was understanding that it was just as much an economic and political issue.

If what I'm saying sounds shockingly naïve to those who know far more about this subject, that is exactly my point. When we are handed the standard version of history without being encouraged to question it, we are set up to be passive listeners more than active participants. We simplify what happened and thus elevate some of it while denying the rest. We idealize key players while suppressing other players' points of view.

The same is true with regard to our individual histories. When we don't come to grips with the complexity of our personal history and the key players in it, we tend to idealize what happened and the people involved or else deny it and dismiss them. We don't want to have to see that what happened did happen and that we cannot undo it. We may fall into trying to rectify the past, to make it better, or to remake it into our own version, but none of these paths sustains curiosity and a quest for truth. From my personal experience and from what I've seen in the therapy room, the only freeing way to deal with an uncomfortable past is to grieve it and thereby retrieve our capacity to be more honest about both past and present.

One of the traps of not looking the past squarely in the eye is what Sigmund Freud called "repetition compulsion," which has to do with repeating harmful or traumatic circumstances again and again. People are typically unaware of how much the past lives inside them and how it drives them unconsciously to act out its imprint and thus repeat the past. When we repeat the past, we stay in earlier habitual responses, which can feel comfortable and familiar; they can also be and feel reliable, even if the results always end up feeling negative and empty.

Sometimes we hold the unconscious hope that if we find ourselves with someone who is similar to a key person from a traumatic past, we can make the past better by doing things differently this time; it's like having a second chance. However, this hope ignores the power of old patterning. One of my clients, Danny, whose father had physically abused him, came out as gay at twenty years old and spent the next decade and a half moving in and out of relationships with men who were emotionally abusive. I met him when he was thirty-five. Over the course of several sessions, we discovered that he actually missed his father even though the relationship had been so abusive. As he uncovered and then worked through his feelings of hate yet love toward his father, Danny became able to choose a partner more carefully. When he found himself tempted to move into what was sure to be an abusive connection, he could recognize it and consciously decide to retreat—he had a choice.

We often see repetition compulsion at play in instances where a person who was abused in childhood swears to never lay a hand on his or her own child, only to end up mimicking much of the behavior of his or her abuser. Feelings of helplessness in the face of danger are among the most traumatic of human experiences. Sometimes the person who has had such experiences yearns, consciously or unconsciously, to one day be the one with more power over another in an intimate relationship, as if this might "cure" the earlier helplessness.

I saw a version of this with Jessica, who came into therapy when she was contemplating a second marriage, which was prompting her to feel intense anxiety. She didn't want to remarry until she was sure her new husband would get along well with her seventeen-year-old daughter, Elizabeth, who had recently been hospitalized for a suicidal episode. After a week of inpatient treatment, Elizabeth was referred to another therapist. The agreement was that I would do family sessions with the two of them, as needed, alongside Jessica's private sessions with me.

Jessica told me that Elizabeth was blaming her for too much—for the divorce, even for Elizabeth's suicide attempt. In a session when both were present, Elizabeth insisted that her father had traumatized her but her mother hadn't protected her. Jessica argued that Elizabeth was overreacting, that her father had only yelled at Elizabeth, not hit her, and anyway, she had already apologized to Elizabeth multiple times. Their relationship was at an impasse—Elizabeth sullen, Jessica frustrated.

When I asked Jessica if this kind of arguing had happened in her family of origin, she thought a moment and said that her parents were religious Christians and had been strict with their children. They talked a lot about hell and were adamant about everyone in the family putting on a happy face, being grateful for what they had, and understanding they had nothing to complain about.

When I encouraged Jessica in her private sessions to delve further into her experience with her parents' hyperactive "happiness gland," as she called it, she accused me of overemphasizing what was already past. She could see no connection between her own childhood history and her relationship with Elizabeth—that is, until she visited her parents one evening and opened up to them about Elizabeth's depression and suicidal ideation. She told me later that she was shocked when her mother said, "When will that girl feel the gratitude she owes you?" Jessica realized at that moment how feeling endlessly pressured to "appreciate all she had" as a child was repeating itself in her own pressuring of Elizabeth to stop being so sensitive. She then looked directly at me and said, "Maybe you weren't as off the mark as I thought."

Although there is no predictability in therapy since we are all so different, Jessica's process was typical in that we tend at first to fight difficult information about our past. We sense that it may be destabilizing, since our past holds our identity and our sense of belonging. Jessica also pushed back with me because she felt guilty for not remaining loyal to her parents, that is, for questioning the rightness of acting happy and grateful when she really wasn't. Yet it was remembering her own history that allowed Jessica to feel her feelings rather than being compelled to bury them and then repeat them in her relationship with her daughter. As she started to own up to her sadness as a child and then to grieve the lack of understanding from her parents, we both began to notice a softening of her feelings toward Elizabeth. She was able to identify with and accept Elizabeth as she was and to apologize to her, not in the hurried and resentment-fraught ways she had previously, but for real.

Facing what has been experienced as pain and cannot be undone can hurt. It can feel like sinking into a bottomless despair from which there is no exit. In fact, there is an exit, but it takes us through the process of mourning. To mourn the past is to embrace the loss of the chances we didn't have, the rapport we didn't have. Sometimes we need to grieve relationships we idealized that we now see were abusive. This is complex, since to grieve the abusive parts means sorting through painful memories that are mixed up with happy ones. Still, as we mourn, we are moving along the hard journey toward change. In the best of circumstances, we can own our positive and negative experiences with key figures in our past, neither idealizing them nor hating them. Perhaps we can then, if intermittently, see them and their flaws with more sobriety and also compassion.

As we become available to accepting new information about our history, we have to be ready to be wrong about the version of history we know. The tools and the supports must be in place to help us deal emotionally with what we discover. We need to be able to process the feelings that show up, especially the emotional impact of finding out we were wrong.

Kathryn Schulz, in her book *Being Wrong: Adventures in the Margin of Error*, talks about exactly this. Schulz appreciates that being wrong, along with the fear of it, is ultimately an emotional experience. Culturally, being wrong is judged as bad, as a defect almost. It is often used as a reason for humiliation rather than being viewed as a natural part of discovery and learning, as it is in science. Schulz says, "If we assume that people who are wrong are ignorant, or idiotic, or evil—well, small wonder that we prefer not to confront the possibility of error in ourselves."[19] This is a reversed variant of the way we project what is in our shadows onto others: instead of seeing our flaws in other people, we see in others something we assume to be a flaw and then refuse to recognize the corresponding part in ourselves.

In our culture's current human climate, where the appearance of certainty is respected above truth, the tendency is to keep our distance from those we see as wrong. We dismiss them out of hand, which leads to an atmosphere of conflict and animosity. People who are so afraid to be wrong tend to insist that what they believe must be real. In speaking of our political leaders, Schulz comments, "We are more alarmed by leaders who waver than by those who screw up."[20]

When we don't want to know that we screwed up, not far behind is the refusal to know that the people before us screwed up—especially when our identity, as citizens or as a nation, depends on glorifying our nation's beginnings and maintaining that glorified image today. The disposition to distance ourselves from our past began with the first people who immigrated from Europe to the "New" World, as if their lives would start all over again once they reached these shores.

According to novelist and historian Wallace Stegner as cited by Kay Redfield Jamison in her book *Exuberance: The Passion for Life*, "History was part of the baggage we threw overboard when we launched ourselves into the New World. We threw it away because it recalled old tyrannies, old limitations, galling obligations, bloody memories. Plunging into the future through a landscape that had no history, we did both the country and ourselves some harm along with some good. Neither the country nor the society we built out of it can be healthy until we stop raiding and running, and learn to be quiet part of the time, and acquire the sense not of ownership but of belonging."[21]

The American (white) exceptionalism of the eighteenth and nineteenth centuries morphed into the right to feel superior to other nations in the twentieth century, in the form of possessing a democracy (though without equality for nonwhites and women) seen as the best in the world. We assumed the right to lead others or else fight with them for a leadership position. Meanwhile, we could feel strong and proud, brave and free—and morally

superior—without questioning whether there was substance behind such arrogance or whether there was blood
on our hands. The price of this optimism and pride was
ignoring the ties to the past. And, as George Santayana
famously wrote, "Those who cannot remember the past
are condemned to repeat it."[22]

On the other hand, some people look to history hoping
to find ways of repeating it as if word for word. They become caught up in the fantasy that we can make the world
better today by reconstructing the conditions of yesterday.
Looking back in time and seeing what is there through
rose-colored glasses, they view the past as comforting, secure, and something to be proud of. Russian-born Svetlana Boym, author of *The Future of Nostalgia*, identifies this
trend as nostalgia. She explains, "Nostalgia (from *nostos*—
return home, and *algia*—longing), is a longing for a home
that no longer exists or has never existed. Nostalgia is a
sentiment of loss and displacement, but it is also a romance with one's own fantasy."[23]

Boym, a former professor of Slavic and comparative
literature at Harvard as well as a gifted artist and novelist,
talks about two kinds of nostalgia: reflective and restorative. Reflective nostalgia is somewhat fluid, a way of
dipping into tradition and coming back out of it. It involves longing for the past but without taking that longing
literally. For instance, when you visit a "retro" restaurant
and listen to 1950s music and let the ethos of that time

wash over you, you enjoy the sentimentality for the evening, but then you come back to the present. Restorative nostalgia is the glorification of the past and the insistence on repeating it. This kind of nostalgia tends to surface in periods of intense cultural uncertainty, when moving forward seems fraught with risk and insecurity. It can lead to regression, to oversimplification, and to attempts to recreate what was, much of which becomes fantasy.

Comparing the two, Boym says that restorative nostalgia "does not think of itself as nostalgia, but rather as truth and tradition. Reflective nostalgia dwells on the ambivalences of human longing and belonging and does not shy away from the contradictions of modernity. Restorative nostalgia protects the absolute truth, while reflective nostalgia calls it into doubt."[24]

Boym also points out that restorative nostalgia "is at the core of recent national and religious revivals; it knows two main plots—the return to origins and the conspiracy."[25] I recognized what she was describing when I came across several articles about Josef Stalin's reputation being "rehabilitated" in Russia. It seems that Vladimir Putin has tried to revive Russian patriotism by reminding Russians that Stalin was responsible for the defeat of Germany during World War II—while ignoring his atrocious war crimes. Mary Chastain of *Breitbart News* commented: "Under leader Vladimir Putin, Soviet dictator Josef Stalin, who purged between 20 and 60 million of his own people, has become increasingly popular in Russia."[26] This is an acute example of restorative nostalgia at work. It is reviving the past without learning from it, its complexity, and its horrific and traumatic downsides.

In case we feel a bit smug about pointing out what's going wrong in Russia, we need only remember the persistent presence of racism in the United States and that none of us are not involved in it. The astute African American author James Baldwin commented in his 1962 essay "Letter from a Region in My Mind" that during World War II, white people were shocked to see Nazis—white people—being so intensely cruel toward other white people, the Jews. He noted that black people, who had experienced gratuitous and planned cruelty at the hands of whites, could imagine it all too well and were not shocked.

In his essay, Baldwin also had something to say about the importance of black people coming to terms with their history. He said it in words that apply to all of us, regardless of color: "The paradox—and a fearful paradox it is—is that the American Negro can have no future anywhere, on any continent, as long as he is unwilling to accept his past. To accept one's past—one's history—is not the same thing as drowning in it; it is learning how to use it."[27]

We all—blacks, whites, everyone—have to face whatever legacy we inherit from the people who came before us, and this can be hard. Baldwin's advice to learn how to use one's history seems to mean not living perpetually as a victim of it. In other words, if we can process the facts as we know them and process our feelings about those facts, we can begin to talk about and listen to and take in what happened. If we can then look together at how the dynamics of the past play out today and set about to repair damages, we will be using history for the good. And if we find out we have been wrong, perhaps about a lot of things, we would do well to be ready to be affected, even changed, by it. Then we could evolve for real.

9
Having a Heart

In the preceding chapters, we have seen how blocked and skipped-over emotions can become congested and prevent us from thinking and feeling clearly. In other words, if we are emotionally congested, we can't think straight or make effective decisions. After writing those chapters, which meant immersing myself in the actual experiences they contain, I found that caring showed up in me as a deeper set of feelings. I realized then that when we do the work of decongesting our emotions, caring is likely to come forth organically. We discover that we have a heart that is beating and that cares.

To care is to make the good of all, not just the good of oneself and one's own, a priority. In a human climate where dividedness holds sway, we are reluctant to really listen to other views or to compromise our own position in order to solve our collective problems. Winning whatever the deal or issue or vote happens to be becomes more important.

I believe that the missing but necessary ingredient for resolving our differences and healing our planet is caring—not just caring from a distance but caring *with*, which is compassion.

I used to think of compassion as feeling sorry for other people who are less well off. However, this superficial sense of the word belies its root meaning of "co-suffering" or "suffering with" (from the Latin *com-pati*). Compassion is more than feeling sorry for others. It is feeling the pain or sorrow of another, sometimes accompanied by the willingness to help. In other words, compassion isn't easy; it calls for going through the discomfort of giving a shit.

It also calls for going through the work of owning our own shadows and flaws. When we face ourselves, when we come up against our own imperfections, when we get to know better our stories and our emotions without rejecting them and without shame, a door opens. We become less judgmental about ourselves. We find more compassion for ourselves, and so it becomes easier to be less judgmental about others, to feel compassion for them and what they have gone through. We don't have to love what everyone does, but to get along we have to understand where they are coming from. They may have started from a place we need to know more about. This approach comes with a feedback loop, since the more compassion we feel toward others, the better we feel about ourselves.

In his book *Just Mercy: A Story of Justice and Redemption*, Bryan Stevenson, a lawyer and founder of the Equal Justice Initiative in Montgomery, Alabama, talks of how the fact that we are flawed makes possible our compassion. He says,

> We are all broken by something. . . . Sometimes we're fractured by the choices we make; sometimes we're shattered by things we would never have chosen. But our brokenness is also the source of our common humanity, the basis for our shared search for comfort, meaning and healing. Our shared vulnerability and imperfection nurtures and sustains our capacity for compassion.
>
> We have a choice. We can embrace our humanness, which means embracing our broken natures and the compassion that remains our best hope for healing. Or we can deny our brokenness, forswear compassion, and, as a result, deny our humanity.[28]

We shy away from acknowledging our own weaknesses, our flaws, our shadows for fear we'll find them too painful. Yet in denying this part of ourselves, we also lose the opportunity to weave a web of connectedness with others that could move us through the kinds of crises, both global and interpersonal, we face today.

Compassion is certainly not a feeling we conjure to feel good about ourselves, even if some authors and experts present it that way. In the current culture, where it seems everything is available for commodification, I have seen articles on the Internet, for instance, that treat compassion as a product or a tool for vitalizing your life.[29] I'll share the problem I have with this marketing of compassion. Compassion is not a strategy to achieve happiness or success. It is a genuine response to facing inconvenient truths about ourselves and others. Compassion is not a smiley face. It calls for going deep, far past surface platitudes. It means being assertive, committed, dedicated, open-hearted, and open-minded—with no guarantee that your actions will be rewarded. It's about being safe and supported enough on the inside to weather the storms of unpredictability that life brings.

~

A human climate tends to hold rules about which experiences and behaviors deserve compassion and which ones don't. Even though we all deserve compassion just for being human, and even more compassion if we are in pain, because of these standards sometimes people who are hurting not only don't receive compassion but receive the opposite. Suffering is hard enough, but being humiliated for suffering adds hardship onto hardship. When this happens often enough that a person anticipates being shamed for being in distress, he or she may deny the pain or try to hide it.

The cultural rules around compassion include assumptions about the respectability of mental illness. Mark Vonnegut, a pediatrician, son of the late Kurt Vonnegut, and someone who was hospitalized four times for psychotic breakdowns, writes in his memoir, *Just*

Like Someone without Mental Illness Only More So, about the artificial bestowing of dignity on the so-called mentally well. "What so-called normal people are doing when they define disease like manic depression or schizophrenia is reassuring themselves that they don't have a thought disorder or affective disorder, that their thoughts and feelings make perfect sense."[30] While a diagnosis can be helpful in therapy and even in daily encounters with people who are suffering, labels can be divisive. The more you get to know a person, the more you see the person outside of the diagnosis. No one shows up exactly the same way all the time.

Among the markers of mental health are a sense of humor and the capacity to witness one's own behavior, and in his writing, Vonnegut displays both. He is witty, sardonic, sometimes passionate and vulnerable as he visits his past and present. He can border on hilarious, such as when he describes being taken in a straitjacket by ambulance to Massachusetts General Hospital, where he was working at the time. He wonders: Couldn't they at least have taken me to a hospital where I was not on staff?

While mental illness can be serious, small breakdowns and falling apart a little are part of being normal and part of growth. Watch a child who is, say, two and a half. There is so much new learning going on as the child puts together concepts for the first time. Yet when we look past the cuteness, we see little breakdowns happening at junctures throughout the day. When a child is moody and tired, for instance, whatever is going on can cause a crush of emotions to pour in, prompting inconsolable crying.

A child having a tantrum can be alarming, as the child looks fragile in such moments. Yet emotional storms are part of the process of growing up. The child gradually learns to get through moments of overwhelming emotionality, and when it is available, to get the support to do so.

For adults, breaking down in little ways can be part of transitional moments, too. When we take in new information or a new way of looking at things, some part of ourselves necessarily breaks a little. Some of our defenses might have to be shed. This can feel unsteadying, even if we understand it as a temporary state on the way to greater stability. The process is not always neat and clean; it can feel kind of crazy and unreliable. Humanizing these experiences is a way of offering dignity, whether it is ourselves or others who are going through these hard times. It equalizes the human playing field as well.

The rules of a particular human climate may include the belief that compassion is a limited-quantity item, that only some people, or certain people, deserve to experience it while others do not. Without even realizing it, we can go along with these conclusions about who is and who is not worthy of compassion and thus find ourselves stuck in fighting over the right to be cared about.

For a while, I worked with two sisters, both in their twenties, who hadn't spoken to each other in months. They hadn't had much experience in resolving differences, and now each was blaming the other for the lack of communication. They had little empathy for each other, and neither of them would tolerate my having empathy for the other sister.

During their growing-up years, their parents had engaged, on and off, in verbal abuse in front of them. Leslie had been the more assertive sister, yelling back at their parents when the fighting began and sometimes becoming entangled in their arguing. Terri, the shy sister, seemed to have it more together, as she would quietly leave the room when the shouting started. However, she shared in therapy that inwardly she had experienced the pain of isolation and feeling left out.

At first, Leslie was furious at me. How dare I be equally empathic with her sister? Didn't I see that she, Leslie, deserved compassion because she had been the one to stick her neck out to protest their parents' fighting and gotten in trouble for it while Terri had done nothing?

The answer was yes, I did see that. I even saw how she had felt abandoned by her sister because Terri didn't validate her when she voiced grievances that were Terri's as well. But, I explained, I also saw how Terri had felt paralyzed by her own fears, which propelled her to flee from situations that were violent emotionally or threatened to become so, and that this called for compassion too.

Leslie was resentful for a while, and Terri too easily took on the role of the guilty sibling who did not deserve compassion because she had been so quiet. In fact, both craved being validated as right. It took a bit of work to get through to them that neither sister was the worthier sufferer. Each had done the best she could and both were worthy of the same degree of empathy for what they had experienced.

As this started to sink in, they could each reach out to the other one, using nicknames that toned down the seriousness of their division: "Hi, fighter," Terri would say. "Hi, flighter," Leslie would offer back. They gradually moved beyond who deserved compassion and began to find a generosity of spirit that helped them stop measuring what each one was receiving and start feeling better about themselves.

Compassion is not something most of us feel immediately on meeting someone; it tends to show up gradually as we listen to the person tell his or her story. This point was underscored for me as I heard Christian Picciolini, cofounder of Life After Hate, interviewed on the radio.[31] The organization Life After Hate helps people who are susceptible to involvement in criminally violent right-wing cult groups find other ways of expressing themselves. Picciolini himself, as a fourteen-year-old, had been lonely and a likely target for any group offering certainty and belonging, so he had joined a right-wing group, eventually becoming one of the group's leaders. Part of what prompted him to change course was when he looked into the eyes of a black kid he was beating up one day and saw the humanness there.

I was intrigued to hear Picciolini tell the interviewer, David Greene, that his most useful tool in engaging with an at-risk person is listening—in particular, listening for the person's emotional experience. He said that when we are present to hear the other person with authentic empathy, we give him or her a chance to open up. There may be a moment to ask a question or make a suggestion, but even to find that moment calls for empathic listening, not assuming we know what the other person needs. Listening with assumptions is not compassion; it lacks the "co," the "feeling with." It can be hard to listen with compassion to people who have committed violent acts. For that matter, it can be hard to listen with compassion to people who have committed ugly acts, or at least acts ugly according to our value system and perception. However, hearing a person describe not only the ugly act he or she did but also how he or she came to do it can be amazing in its power to transform us, the listeners. It offers us an opportunity to make space to feel the emotional truth of another human being, and, some of the time, the judgmental, disgusted attitude we may have had about that person just hours before can shift into a more humanizing outlook.

As it turns out, the more we travel to and through our shadows, the more likely we are to discover our heart, which is waiting to open up in caring. Compassion is potentially present in all of us, sitting under the congestion and the habits that have grown out of that congestion. Tapping into that compassion doesn't make our road any simpler. However, it does help us to allow each other and our world to matter—to allow ourselves to care more. I sense that underneath our defensive stances we all do actually yearn to let down our pretenses, to share our humanity, our mistakes, our fears. If we could do that, our human climate would surely be different.

10
In Support of Not Knowing

I would have liked in this final chapter to write a dramatic conclusion of some kind. But given that this book is an effort to see into arguably some of the most challenging issues we face, it's not possible to reach for honesty and at the same time tie everything up with a bow. Instead, this chapter explores one more topic that is every bit as important as having a heart at a time when the human climate is so polarized: the importance of not knowing.

Underscoring this entire writing endeavor is the question: Can and will we, as a nation and a species, evolve further so we don't kill the world? It is no longer enough for us to adapt to existing circumstances. Rather, we need to get beyond at least some of the divisions that have marked our world for many years now and threaten to for many years more.

I believe that to achieve this shift, we as people, both individually and collectively, need to shift. I like to say that we need to *be growing up*, since we are works in progress and not done, not "grown up." It is never possible to grow up completely because life keeps presenting us with new experiences and challenges, and we need to continue becoming the beings who can meet those experiences and challenges as best we can.

Continuing to grow means continuing to learn. A child reaches a certain level of development, but then the next lesson comes along and the child must feel awkward and ignorant again while learning it. So also, we may draw a certain conclusion, but then someone brings a new point or fact to our attention, and even if we are recognized as experts, we have to come up against our not knowing again.

Not much can be resolved or solved about any dilemma without finding out as much as we can about it. In other words, the truth is important. By "truth" here I mean objective truth, such as the fact that the annual average temperature of the earth is rising, or the fact that a certain adult hit a certain child. This is in contrast to subjective truth, which is true for the person making the judgment but not necessarily true for others. For example, one person sitting in a room may feel overheated and say "It's too hot in here," while everyone else finds the temperature quite comfortable. Both are important, but here I mean especially objective truth.

Even our ability to know what is objectively true is conditioned by time, place, culture, and even personality style and intelligence, all of which are filters that color what we perceive. Even so, people committed to truth will continually seek to add to or refine their understanding. This means being willing at times to admit to not knowing.

People tend to avoid positions of not knowing. It can be easier or more comfortable to take on the appearance of knowing even when one doesn't. Sometimes it's strategic to pass for strong and invulnerable. Sometimes getting what one is after becomes more important than the terms—the lies—it takes. This is what philosopher Harry Frankfurt calls "bullshit."

In his incisive little book *On Bullshit*, Frankfurt defines the term by comparing it with speaking the truth and out-and-out lying. He writes, "When an honest man speaks, he says only what he believes to be true; and for the liar, it is correspondingly indispensable that he considers his statements to be false. For the bullshitter, however, all these bets are off: he is neither on the side of the true nor on the side of the false. His eye is not on the facts at all. . . . He does not care whether the things he says describe reality correctly. He just picks them out, or makes them up, to suit his purpose."[32]

In fact, bullshitting can happen quite innocuously. As Frankfurt writes, "Bullshit is unavoidable whenever circumstances require someone to talk without knowing what he is talking about."[33] As an example: I ask a question of a friend and expect him to answer me. He may not actually have an answer, but he feels obliged to respond anyway, so he comes up with a response just to get on with the conversation. He surrenders the truth for the sake of appearing as though he knows.

The pressure we feel to appear smart about things we are not smart about can be insidious. In the case of my friend, I would argue that he would have served us both better if he had paused a moment, noticed the pressure he felt to say something, and spoken honestly, saying that he didn't know but maybe he could find out later and let me know, or we could find out together. I also recognize that his response could happen to most of us, if for no other reason than people can't be expected to know about so much.

However, in bullshitting's more egregious forms, there is no loyalty to honesty; the person wants to make an impression or win a point, not help solve a problem. This means that we can't trust the information of someone who is bullshitting us, nor can we trust his or her motivations. When people who are trying to tell the truth realize they are wrong, they will do their best to make amends and change course. But a producer of bullshit—whether a doctor or lawyer or politician or lover, even—wants solely to convince us of their point of view and so will persist at any cost.

In the current era of increasing polarization, socially and politically, both sides have come to expect that the other side is bullshitting them. Neither side expects to be persuaded by the other; in fact, they arm themselves with defenses to prevent that from happening and then do battle, relative truth to relative truth.

When positions harden to the point where there are fixed sides, there is no way to collaborate and talk out loud to come to a solution together. Everything becomes about winning, about being on a team where we can be right together. When I had the opportunity to explore this issue with Kyle Saunders, associate professor of political science at Colorado State University, he talked about the role that "team feeling" plays in political polarization and how "affective partisanship," the mutual dislike between Republicans and Democrats, has been on the rise since the 1970s. The word "affective" caught my ear, since it acknowledges the central role emotions play in current politics. Strength is counted in numbers and in terms of who has the upper hand, rather than in truth. In the United States, anyway, we're supposed to be living in a democracy, but democracy is impossible without collaboration and cooperation. It feels more like we are in a state of civil war, though one fought mostly with language and ideas.

To find out what is true, we have to know we can trust the experts and specialists who say and show us that they have access to at least some bits of objective truth. We have to find out if they are able (and willing) to say they don't know when that is the case. For if they too are willing to bullshit us, how can we trust what they say as true?

Part of getting to the truth and away from bullshit has to do with recognizing what we don't know, which can help us be more open to asking for support or opinion from others. At the very least, it can help us recognize something new that comes our way and take it in if it seems urgent. We have, of course, an easier time doing so when we are already more open than not.

As this book's author, I'm inspired to do my part in admitting that I don't know, that I am in the course of trying to find things out instead of knowing for sure. Just as vulnerability is often more naked and sudden than it is beautiful and poetic, it doesn't feel so good to say "I don't know" out loud. Yet admitting what we don't know or are confused about might just be a refreshing beginning of better communication. It might even be exactly what we need right now, because much of life is confusing—and to admit that is to admit reality.

Although there is a lot that we as individuals don't know about, each of us also has information and experience to offer. If we can take a step back and admit we don't know, we can begin to be open to each other's thoughts and opinions. The truth is that we need each other's help to be better informed—and we can help each other if our motivation is not to win at every juncture but rather to listen, learn, and support one another. As I have been saying, this can happen only when we address the divisions within us by humanizing all of our emotions.

With less divisiveness inside us, we might be better able to see our fundamental connectedness with all the other people on the planet, and with the natural world as well, and to embrace the fact that any honest quest for knowledge must involve opening doors to what others have to say.

Certainly every person's view counts, since ultimately, we have to face the future together. Several years ago, when this book was only an idea, I shared some of my thoughts about the human climate with an experienced clinical psychologist. He expressed interest in the concept, so I asked if he'd like to collaborate. He responded that the idea was fascinating and pertinent but then added, "It's just that it's not my field." In other words, he acknowledged that he didn't know—but then he used his lack of knowledge as a reason not to engage.

I have to say that I found his comment shocking. It was a bit like asking a person if he or she believes in God and getting the same answer: "It's not my field." Isn't the God question everybody's field?

Trite as it may sound to say it, we truly are all in this together. We all matter. We're all affected by each other. As such, we're obligated to care, even if we can offer no more than an honest "I don't know." After all, in the story of the emperor's new clothes, it was a young boy who said, in essence, "I don't see what the rest of you say you're seeing." His giving voice to his own experience (his honest experience at that) made others aware of their own experience, thereby creating space for them to recognize what they were seeing: their revered leader was naked.

As you can guess, it's my fervent opinion that the human climate is everybody's field and that we each have something to contribute, whether it's our need for help or our capacity to give it, since we are likely to spend some time in both positions. After all, we are all on and in the same field in the sense of sharing the physical space of the planet.

We all need supports, people who will teach us strategies and people who will support us while we practice talking out loud and having boundaries. And we need to increase the sense that cooperation for the greater good is possible and can even be exciting. We may love to hate (remember the shadows) and be addicted to the same, but if we comb through those shadows and get to know what is there, we may free up our excitement for play and invention.

Though sanity is apparently a relative, not absolute, condition (as we saw in the case of Mr. Vonnegut in chapter 9), it is a condition we can aspire to and even achieve to a fair degree, if only partially and sometimes. I would argue that an aspect of sanity is recognition that you don't know everything, and it follows that it's insane to say you know when you don't. Even though it can feel threatening to say "I don't know," we're likely to know a lot more when we're willing to say it. We may realize what we do know, or we may allow a creative process to emerge and its revelations to surprise us.

When we can give up the grandiose ownership of a stilted imitation of sanity, we reach the kind of "brokenness" discussed by Bryan Stevenson: the breaking down of insisting on our habitual way of thinking and doing things. We become broken open enough to become caring toward others and what they have to teach us, even as we muster enough gentleness for ourselves so that we don't take to resenting the brokenness of not knowing. This may lead us to a more fluid use of the term "sanity," one that includes enough emotional flexibility, awareness, and integration to allow thought to function alongside opinion.

There is a close relationship between sanity and health, as the language shows. "Sanity" and "sanitation" are from the same Latin root, *sanitas* or *sanus*. So also, *sanità* is the Italian word for health. And *à la santé* is a toast in French: "To health."

"To our sanity" is my toast, followed by a toast to a lighter time when we will stop living in these "darker ages" during which people have purposely turned out the lights on knowledge. And then, a toast to our shadows. May they inform us and become integrated with the other parts of us, so the divisions within us lessen as well. And, of course, a final toast: To us. May we judge ourselves less harshly.

Notes

1. Neil Genzlinger, "Mapping Out a Holiday with the Family: Staging 'A Beautiful Day in November on the Banks of the Greatest of the Great Lakes,'" *New York Times*, January 8, 2015.

2. Carol Smaldino, "White Liberal Racism: An Interview with Dr. Robin DiAngelo," *Huffington Post*, August 18, 2016.

3. Bruno Bettelheim, *The Uses of Enchantment: The Meaning and Importance of Fairy Tales* (New York: Knopf, 1976), p. 66.

4. Michael Chabon, *The Amazing Adventures of Kavalier and Clay* (New York: Picador, 2000), p. 474.

5. Ibid., p. 552.

6. Greg Jemsek, *Quiet Horizon: Releasing Ideology and Embracing Self-Knowledge* (Bloomington, IN: Trafford, 2011), p. 54.

7. Annette Stephens, *The Good Little Girl* (New South Wales: Big Sky Publishing, 2012).

8. Carl Jung, *The Undiscovered Self* (New York: Little, Brown, 1957), pp. 104–5.

9. Ibid., p. 98.

10. Ibid., p. 96.

11. Ibid., p. 100.

12. Martin E.P. Seligman, *Authentic Happiness: Using the New Positive Psychology to Realize Your Potential for Lasting Fulfillment* (New York: Free Press, 2002), p. 67.

13. Barbara Ehrenreich, "Smile! You've Got Cancer," *Guardian*, January 1, 2010.

14. Barbara Ehrenreich, *Bright-Sided: How Positive Thinking Is Undermining America* (New York: Henry Holt and Company, 2010), p. 146.

15. Richard Hofstadter, *The American Political Tradition and the Men Who Made It* (New York: Vintage Books, 1989), p. 150.

16. Ibid., p. 150, footnote.

17. Ibid., p. 149.

18. Ibid.

19. Kathryn Schulz, *Being Wrong: Adventures in the Margins of Error* (New York: HarperCollins, 2010), p. 110.

20. Ibid., p. 174.

21. Wallace Stegner, *Where the Bluebird Sings to the Lemonade Springs* (New York: Random House, 1992), p. xx, quoted in Kay Redfield Jamison, *Exuberance: The Passion for Life* (New York: Knopf, 2004), pp. 250–251.

22. George Santayana, *The Life of Reason: Reason in Common Sense* (New York: Scribner, 1905), p. 284.

23. Svetlana Boym, *The Future of Nostalgia* (New York: Basic Books, 2001), p. xiii.

24. Ibid., p. xiii.

25. Ibid., p. xviii.

26. Mary Chastain, "Under Vladimir Putin, Josef Stalin's Popularity on the Rise in Russia," *Breitbart News*, December 22, 2015; see also Alec Luhn, "Stalin, Russia's New Hero," *The New York Times*, March 11, 2016.

27. James Baldwin, "Letter from a Region in My Mind," excerpts published in *The New Yorker*, February 21, 2000.

28. Bryan Stevenson, *Just Mercy: A Story of Justice and Redemption* (New York: Spiegel and Grau, 2014), p. 289.

29. See, for example, Jen Christensen, "Want to Be Happy and Successful? Try Compassion," CNN website, June 11, 2017. Available at http://edition.cnn.com/2017/04/12/health/compassion-happiness-training/index.html.

30. Mark Vonnegut, *Just Like Someone without Mental Illness Only More So* (New York: Bantam Books, 2011), p. 166.

31. Christian Picciolini, interview by David Greene, NPR *Morning Edition*, April 25, 2017.

32. Harry Frankfurt, *On Bullshit* (Princeton: Princeton University Press, 2005), p. 56.

33. Ibid., p. 63.

CPSIA information can be obtained
at www.ICGtesting.com
Printed in the USA
FSHW011736011218
53994FS